"As a father o efforts to help parents and teachers guide our future men to a brighter tomorrow."

-Gerry Robert,
Bestselling Author of *The Millionaire Mindset*

"Winning back our Boys is like an answer to the 911 call that parents and teachers have been frantically dialing. It gives practical, yet powerful solutions that can be used in everyday situations by adults dealing with young men."

-Frederick Williams
Retired Professor of African American Studies
University of Texas San Antonio

"*Winning Back Our Boys* is a valuable new contribution to the small but growing genre of books concerned with the essential psychological, educational, social, and parenting needs of boys and young men. It is very well-researched and written with clarity and passion. It gives anyone concerned about the well-being of boys useful insights and helpful guidance."

-Aaron Kipnis, PhD.,
Author of *Angry Young Men: How Parents, Teachers, and Counselors can Help "Bad Boys" Become Good Men.*

"Cannon is a hero at the front lines of saving our boys. In clear and direct language, propelled by common sense and compassion, Cannon offers solutions which will help us to win back our boys and secure for them a safe and successful future."

-Cary Clack,
Columnist for San Antonio Express-News

"It is rare that I read an entire book in one day. However, I could not put this book down. It communicated so much vital information in a very interesting and powerful way that I was compelled to keep reading it to the end. Mr. Cannon puts forth a plethora of sobering facts regarding the forces that are impacting our youth today. The good news is, Cannon does not stop there, but he shares useful tools that any parent can immediately put into practice with their children. It is easy to talk about what's wrong with the world, but it takes a man of courage to challenge you and show you what you can do about it. Although I do not have any children, I was deeply impacted by this book."

-Chef Tracey, San Antonio, Texas

"Chris Cannon explains why so many of our young men get into trouble starting at early ages and writes a prescription for how to stop this epidemic. Anyone interested in the future of our children, our educational system or our society in general will not be able to put this book down."

-Beatrice Tumbleweed, Montana

"As a man who has witnessed firsthand the cultural war that is being waged against our nation's youth, it is truly refreshing to know that 'watchmen' like Chris Cannon are still manning their posts. From his perspective as a national youth advocate and a passionate father, Cannon boldly unveils the issues and challenges facing children today, while offering practical solutions on how to address them. This book is a vital resource for those who have sons or interact with young men on any level."

-David Mahan, CEO, Frontline Youth Communications, Columbus, Ohio

"Chris Cannon has created a great tool to help in the daily battle of teaching boys to become productive young men. As an employee in an Urban School District, it is plain to see the factors that contribute to young men taking the wrong path. Cannon illuminates the numerous factors, starting from childhood, leading to the mental, emotional and physical destruction of our young men. On a personal level, I was forced to deal with some of my very own personal feelings and the reasons I had them. This book is also a great tool for not only identifying and understanding problems, but for also providing answers and examining root causes. I think every man who works with young men should read this book. Not only to assist and understand, but also to grasp the reasons behind our own insecurities about being productive men in today's world."

-Michael Fleming, High School Teacher, Columbus, Ohio

"This book needs to be in the hands of every educator, principal, superintendent, pastor, youth leader and most of all, every young man struggling to find his place in society. I have been asked to give the public address to a group of school administrators in one of the counties I serve. They are having a back to school rally and all the teachers and administrators will be there. I recommend Cannon's book as mandatory reading material for teachers. I am considering putting together a PowerPoint presentation of what I have learned from the book in order to share Cannon's information with the audience."

-Eric Love, East Texas Youth Program Coordinator

"My 13-year-old son and I read this book independently. This allowed us an opportunity to discuss the material weekly over dinner and stimulated numerous conversations regarding peer pressure, becoming focused, being responsible for one's own actions, notions of manhood and raising our level of expectation. This book definitely raised my level of awareness as well as my son's. We appreciate the effort and the amount of information prepared in the text. The author's work is unique and frank explanations and as a result, my son and I will move through the remainder of the teenage years with greater emphasis on priorities and open communication to assure that he becomes a young man of positive influence."

-Professor Elise Buggs, Ann Arbor, Michigan

WINNING back our
BOYS

The Ultimate Gameplan for Parents & Teachers

WINNING back our BOYS

The Ultimate Gameplan for Parents & Teachers

CHRIS CANNON

All Rights Reserved
© 2010 by Chris Cannon

This book may not be reproduced in whole or in part, by any means, without written consent of the publisher.

LIFESUCCESS PUBLISHING, LLC
8900 E Pinnacle Peak Road, Suite D240
Scottsdale, AZ, 85255

Telephone:	800.473.7134
Fax:	480.661.1014
E-mail:	admin@lifesuccesspublishing.com
ISBN:	978-1-59930-272-0
Cover:	Lloyd Arbour, LifeSuccess Publishing, LLC
Text:	Lloyd Arbour, LifeSuccess Publishing, LLC
Edit:	LifeSuccess Publishing, LLC; AllIvy Editing Services

COMPANIES, ORGANIZATIONS, INSTITUTIONS, AND INDUSTRY PUBLICATIONS. Quantity discounts are available on bulk purchases of this book for reselling, educational purposes, subscription incentives, gifts, sponsorship, or fundraising. Special books or book excerpts can also be created to fit specific needs such as private labeling with your logo on the cover and a message from a VIP printed inside. For more information, please direct all inquiries to info@Fighting4Youth.com.

DEDICATION

I dedicate this book to my Proverbs 31 woman, for all of the sacrifice, encouragement, and unparalleled support she continues to provide me. I also dedicate this book to the two best children God could ever have blessed me with. Devon, thank you for understanding when we couldn't play basketball because of book deadlines or have story time because I needed to write. Arianna, I appreciate your patience while I finished a few paragraphs before playing baby dolls with you in your room. We'll definitely spend more time together now.

For all your patience, support, and understanding, it's my honor to dedicate this book to all of you.

APPLAUSE AND THANKS

I'd like to thank everyone who was a part of the team that made this project a success. All the strategic planning has been more than worth it. Writing a book is, at times, a very frustrating process, to say the least. However, every parent I interviewed brought me encouragement. It was as if each interview was destined for the exact moment and time it took place. Each interview helped me through a different challenge I was facing both personally and in the writing process. Parents, as the information you provided will help others, the process of obtaining the information helped me, and for that I sincerely thank you.

To every youth leader I interviewed for this book, I am honored and grateful for your assistance and support. Each interview contributed a uniqueness that readers will appreciate. Each of your perspectives was different, but all were relevant to the solutions that parents and teachers will implement after this reading experience. I am confident that others will learn from the information you've provided, as I did.

I felt I gained wisdom and insight from aunts and uncles across the country whom I recently met and interviewed. Each of you poured something different in my life that I needed to complete the quest that God has me on. It was as if you communicated something to me that needs to be communicated to the rest of the family. Though none of you know each other, you all have big hearts and compassion for youth and for people in general, which creates a level of connectedness that's stronger than in most families that have known each other for a lifetime. Even though we shared just a brief moment over the phone, you will forever remain in my heart. I'm encouraged and inspired to continue this battle knowing that you are in the trenches in pursuit of victory as well, and for that I sincerely thank you.

CONTENTS

Foreword	15
Introduction	17
1. Good Boys ... Bad Approach *Showing Boys How to Make the Grade*	19
2. The Broken Male *Putting the Emotional Pieces Back Together*	43
3. Sexploitation *The Deception of Manhood and What Has to Be Done to Stop It*	57
4. Stop. Look. Listen. *What Boys Wish Their Parents Knew about Them*	75
5. Escaping the Virtual Trap *Why Wounded Boys Think They're Heroic Men*	99
6. Taking Boys Captive *How Punishment Causes Pain for Some and Profit for Others*	113
7. The Wizard of Oz *Revealing the Secret behind the Screen*	133

8. The Breeding Ground of Success   147
What Parents Are Doing to Get the Results They Want

9. Reporting from the Front Row   171
Action Steps and Advice From the Nation's Youth Leaders

10. The Ultimate Game Plan   201

FOREWORD

As a young man growing up without a father, I was blessed to have people in my life to guide and mentor me during my adolescent years. Chris Cannon a.k.a. "Coach Cannon" was someone you could talk to, relate to and look to for guidance. He would say, "If you ever need something let me know." Many people use this phrase, but very few stand by it. I remember needing a few dollars for my senior prom, but couldn't find anyone to help. Although it was last minute, I called Coach Cannon and he didn't hesitate to help. I knew I could always count on him. To this day, I still remember the kindness that Coach Cannon showed me. He understood where I was from, where I wanted to end up in life and was someone who wanted to see me get there, with no ulterior motive, which is rare. Thanks Coach Cannon!

—James Holmes
Professional European Basketball Player
08/09 Spain

INTRODUCTION

What is the state of young men in America? Young men without ambition, encouragement, and motivation can be detrimental to themselves and to our society as a whole. Statistics show boys are at greater risk than girls for developing learning disabilities, illiteracy, and substance abuse problems; for dropping out of school, having sex, being arrested, and dying young due to violent behavior. As boys grow older, risky behaviors, such as alcohol and drug abuse, become more prevalent, and gang involvement increases. Society seems to fear young boys because of negative stereotypes. *Winning Back Our Boys* illustrates that this need not be the case and demonstrates the need to change that fear.

It is imperative for these young men to find good role models and establish a nurturing relationship with them. We also need to ensure that young men are fully prepared for what today and the future holds for them. When I was a teacher, I saw firsthand the need to help young boys build their self-esteem and know their value. *Winning Back Our Boys* is committed not only to helping young men realize their potential in life, but also to helping parents, educators, and community leaders see it too. By exposing this generation to the positive side of life and fostering an environment of acceptance and success, we can enable them to follow their dreams and benefit society rather than be a burden. To those ends, this book highlights the key factors of education, self-identity, responsibility, parental involvement, and handling the latest technology in a positive way.

It's my sincere hope that as you read through these pages, you gain an understanding of the plight young men face on a daily basis, and how you can help them reach their full potential.

CHAPTER 1

GOOD BOYS ... BAD APPROACH

SHOWING BOYS HOW TO MAKE THE GRADE

CHAPTER 1

Our education system has many commendable characteristics, with one exception in particular. It doesn't address the learning styles of many of our young men, and thus, doesn't meet their needs. This is evident in the disproportionate dropout rate of boys compared to girls, which will be discussed later in this chapter. The majority of teachers have a certain preconceived notion of the ideal student, which hinders many young men. They regard characteristics such as politeness, attentiveness, calmness, quietness, and passiveness, to a certain degree, as desirable. Of course, many of these characteristics are feminine in nature and don't coincide with the behavior of most young men, who are typically active, assertive, physical, visually oriented, and curious. Many times teachers perceive these qualities as unsatisfactory because, often, the display of them disrupts the classroom.

It has been my experience that males predominately are visual learners who have outstanding visual memory. In order to be engaged on an educational level, male minds need physical and visual demonstration. Rather than utilizing this knowledge to enhance male learning, our school systems instead turn this into a weakness through classroom lectures. It's very difficult for young boys to sit still for fifty minutes and listen to their teacher talk without any interaction or visual stimulus to keep their attention, just as it is for adults.

Visual learners remember what they see, but oftentimes they forget what they hear and have difficulty with organizational skills. They operate from the right hemisphere of the brain, which involves the intuitive, creative side of life. Skillful use of symbols and images, face recognition, and imagination are ways they display their strengths. They're outside-the-box thinkers who, when given the opportunity, can come up with numerous solutions to a single problem. Where the left hemisphere sees parts of the whole, the right hemisphere understands the entire, big picture. Neither perspective is less important or wrong. However, the left fits more easily into the traditional education setting and has been rewarded most often in the classroom.

Further, educational systems punish students for their inability to answers questions about subjects they have no previous knowledge of. Students are often given standardized tests with content they are seeing for the first time. Due to many recently mandated requirements, teachers complain of being forced to give tests without the adequate time and materials to prepare students properly. Students are expected to test well on materials that they've never been taught. Much of the new testing that's being required on the local and state levels is on subjects irrelevant in comparison to the material that will further these students' success.

Effective learning is when a person is allowed to make a mistake in a supportive environment and then is given the opportunity to make corrections. The problem today is that young people are driven by the fear of being wrong, instead of by the excitement of learning. The average student feels more afraid than inspired by his teachers because of his fear of failure. In many cases, failing grades are not always the best indicator of a student's skill set, but rather a result of disconnect with the teacher or with the curriculum.

Many famous people who have made significant contributions to society also struggled academically and made several mistakes, but we benefit a great deal every day from their achievements. Among them are Thomas Edison, Henry Ford, Bill Gates, Robert Kiyosaki, Robert Townsend, and Bill Cosby, to name a few. Robert Kiyosaki, author of the "Rich Dad Poor Dad" series of books, was once considered one of the worst students in Hawaii. Most recently, he has become known as one of the greatest financial teachers to ever walk the earth and has taught thousands of people how to become multimillionaires by proving that first impressions are no indicator of future success.

Students often don't grasp the connection between today's homework and tomorrow's professional aspirations and frequently ask, "Why do I need to learn this?" or "How is this going to help in the real world?" When these types of questions remain unanswered in an instructor's teaching, students never see the true relevance in the lessons taught. The student who loves art and desires to pursue it professionally might find it difficult to see the value in studying history—especially if his history teacher doesn't recognize or respect his talent in art and see how it could be related to history. Teachers who implement their students' unique talents and skills into classroom teaching will enrich the learning experience not only of that student in particular but of their classes as a whole.

A history teacher I had the pleasure of speaking to described how one of his students who was struggling in the subject actually made history more interesting for the class while bringing up his own grades in the process. The teacher had the student stay after class for a few minutes and give him a briefing on the lesson for the next class, along with a few pages to read. From this, the student, who was talented in art, drew pictures representing scenes from the teacher's next lesson. The teacher spoke of how effective the technique was, because the rest of the students were eager to see what their classmate would draw next. This increased the young man's confidence in history and allowed him to feel a part of the learning process. The teacher said students often felt as though they were more emotionally involved because they had the visual image complementing the auditory teaching.

If students aren't receiving the correct answers to their questions, the education system should look for other alternatives, such as implementing new curricula and teaching methods or giving the students a learning styles test at the beginning of the school year to meet students' particular needs. When students don't understand why they are learning certain subjects, they tune out and do just enough to get a satisfying grade by memorizing the material, instead of learning it. If they're able to apply the teaching to their life, it's more likely they'll internalize that information, because facts that are understood are retained longer than those that are only memorized.

Oftentimes, teachers give worksheets and other assignments that have no meaning, relevance, or connection to real life. Consequently, many students have stopped asking questions, and some resort to cheating just to get through classes. They've discovered the most important objective in school is not learning, but receiving good grades. Sadly, when students are rewarded for grades, not for what they've learned, cheating becomes the easy answer. This makes classrooms competitive and individualistic, which eliminates the social interaction of learning.

Some students who recognize the emphasized importance of grades stop caring altogether. They see the work as useless and irrelevant to their lives, so they consider dropping out, and many actually do. Boys constitute nearly 80 percent of the dropouts.[1] As an improvement to our educational system, however, some suggest extending class time, or, even worse in my opinion, extending the school year. That's equivalent to giving a trigonometry problem to a child who has never seen trigonometry before and saying, "If you keep it in front of him long enough, he'll figure it out on his own." Doing so would make no sense because it's not relevant to him and it has no connection to his life.

In classroom settings, true teaching time should be a stimulus, not a babysitter. Assignments should be creative work, not just "busy work," and students should question more answers than answer more questions. As students mature and advance in school, the less likely they are encouraged to ask questions, yet the more teachers expect from them. Several studies indicate that the older students get, the less positive they feel about their educational experience.[16] Early elementary school children are generally more interested in school because of their interaction and involvement with their teachers; therefore, they are excited about their education experience. More learning occurs in classes where students have a high degree of involvement. Students are more satisfied in classrooms where participation is encouraged in a variety of activities and where personal relationships are positive.

Teachers today have minimal accountability for contributing to the success of our young men. I'm in no way suggesting that the sole responsibility falls on teachers; rather, I wish to recognize that the level of expectations teachers place on students tremendously impacts their educational success. If students aren't doing well in school, the perception is usually that something is wrong with the student, but rarely that anything is wrong with the teacher or the educational system. Most academic issues that lead to behavioral problems escalate because of teacher responses that discourage rather than encourage; educators have the choice of using their position as an instrument of demoralization or inspiration.

A classic example of this is Jane Elliott, a third-grade teacher in Riceville, Iowa. She completed a study on discrimination by using eye color. Her intent was to show how people feel when they are discriminated against. She started out by telling her students that blue-eyed people are smarter than brown-eyed people. Before the study ended, several of the blue-eyed students believed they were better than the brown-eyed students. They even began to fight one another because one of the students tauntingly called another "brown eyes." The teacher later asked the student why he was upset by being called "brown eyes," and the student said, "Because they [brown-eyed people] are stupid." She then conducted another exercise, this time discriminating against blue-eyed people, making the brown-eyed students feel superior. The exercises taught both groups how it felt to be discriminated against.

A teacher's perception of a student determines his or her expectations from the student. For example, as a teacher I saw firsthand how a student whose older sister or brother attended that school was treated based on what the siblings did, whether bad or good. This is unfair to the younger siblings, who were never given a chance to establish their own reputations, but rather were given one based on the behavior of others.

This is similar to what male students experience in school, but rather than an older sister or brother passing down a reputation, male students are assigned a reputation based on their gender. They're often stereotyped by how they dress or look, and sometimes just by the fact that they're males. Expectations are low, and if they've had any setbacks along the way, expectations fall lower still.

When young men are treated "how they are," they become nothing more, but when treated "how they could be," they become all they can. This is developed only through positive relationships. Teachings that impact lives are not head to head, but heart to heart. A subtle reminder educators should consider is this: It's not important what you do as a teacher, but the importance lies in what the learners do as a result of what they were taught. Questions all teachers should ask themselves include "What do I know?" and "What do I want them to know?" "What do I feel?" and "What do I want them to feel?" "What do I do?" and "What do I want them to do?" These questions, in most cases, go unasked because teachers teach the way they were taught, ignoring the various learning styles children possess and forcing them into a certain style of learning.

Most children who are labeled as having Attention Deficit Disorder (ADD) are right-brained children (a predominately male trait), who are taught predominately by left-brained teachers (a predominately female trait). This is important because those doing the labeling are largely females, who make up the vast majority of teachers.[20] Oftentimes, left-brained teachers teach only from a left-brain perspective because it is what makes them most comfortable. The difference in the learning styles of young men causes them to be perceived as disruptive, problematic, rude, and disrespectful. In most cases, young men's needs are not being met, and teachers who fail to do so never truly understand these students and see what they are capable of producing.

If the energy of young men is channeled in the right direction, it will help them become successful adults who contribute to society. Often, we want boys to sit down and be quiet, but that's not how they're wired. It's hard to encourage young men to be strong when everything we teach them as being "right" removes their strength. The restless behaviors they express in the classroom are often last resorts in trying to express to educators that their educational needs aren't being met.

Young men need creative outlets, such as drawing, music, sports, and any other activity of physical or verbal expression. A large proportion of young boys fall behind girls educationally early on in their schooling, which sometimes intimidates the boys. The way young men cope with this harsh reality is by manipulating the environment in ways that display their strength and self-confidence. Physical strength becomes their weapon to fight the battle of their insecurities in dealing with those they perceive to be more intelligent. They might challenge teachers physically by disrupting class and making statements such as "What are you going to do to me?" This is especially true toward teachers whom they can intimidate with their size. Many times this coping mechanism results in punishment with some form of in-school or out-of-school suspension.

When boys don't understand something or feel they are being ignored or mistreated, they act out. The primary reason is because they would rather be viewed as bad or dangerous than dumb or stupid. They rarely, if ever, feel ashamed at being viewed as bad or dangerous and more often than not take pride in it. Many feel neglected as far as education is concerned because most teachers don't understand how to teach them effectively or teach in a manner that is more geared to females. Since 71 percent of all teachers are female, it's understandable that many young men feel unable to connect with their teachers.[45] This is not to insinuate that female teachers are bad or don't recognize the needs of their male students, but rather to bring awareness to the thought process and actions of young men. When they are asked to make a decision educationally and aren't given the option to express themselves, these young men shut down and stop listening.

Boys and girls mature at different rates but are compared and expected to perform at the same level, especially early in grade school. Many young men are placed in lower levels because they don't perform the same as females, which instantly labels them "at risk." When students are labeled as "vulnerable," "at risk," or "lower level," it singles them out as different. This is equivalent to several people asking you regularly "Are you okay?" or telling you how bad you look. After a while, you're going to start believing something is wrong with you. For this reason, "boys are in the minority for being valedictorians, receiving academic scholarships, and becoming new college students that go onto graduate."[17] Instead, "boys are dropping out more frequently and exhibiting more behavior problems, forcing teachers to spend less time teaching the three R's and more time on the three D's: Drugs, Distractions, and Discipline."[10]

If schools were to offer learning-style tests for their students, much of the negative behavior in boys would be eliminated. These tests provide teachers with the necessary information to gear their teaching style toward various learning needs. Due to the lack of educational concern for boys, however, their learning needs are often overlooked. Males have speech impediments, dyslexia, and other learning disabilities at a significantly higher rate than females.[1] In most cases, these issues are misdiagnosed as behavioral problems, especially when teachers or other adults try to force boys to participate publicly in something "educational" that could expose their weaknesses.

I grew up labeled dyslexic and in elementary school had a hard time making educational progress in certain classroom settings. Although it was clear in my mind that I wasn't going to embarrass myself publicly by participating in specific activities, acting out was not an option for me; my mom had a way of placing fear in me even when she wasn't present. So, the excuse I used to get out of the activity was saying "I don't feel well," and I would ask to go to the bathroom every time I anticipated being called on to read.

The tactic I used is rare; most young men let their anger and frustration control their actions. When they detect that they are about to be exposed or mistreated, they instantly become defensive and reactive. This makes other alternatives attractive for them, such as special education or suspension. Special education is suggested by many mainstream teachers who choose not to deal with the underlying behavioral issues. These recommendations are often based solely on the young men's behavior and not on their academic ability. Boys are placed in special education at a rate that's alarmingly high compared to girls. Among blacks placed in special education, more than 84 percent are males.[43] The rate for males in Latino and Hispanic communities is significantly higher as well. Males and minorities alike are given less time in class to correct wrong answers, compared to higher achieving students. This has a direct connection to the expectations placed on them. When students aren't expected to excel in a particular area, teachers see no point in wasting time.

Unfortunately, when boys are recommended for special education, they're often also given negative labels such as "violent" or "disruptive" and as a result are treated as such. Boys are more likely to be expelled from school for the same act a female has done, mainly because boys are perceived as more of a physical threat to their female teachers. Minorities, especially black males and students from lower socioeconomic backgrounds are suspended at significantly higher rates than females and Caucasian students of middle- and upper-class status. This pattern is widespread. According to the Maryland State Department of Education, Caucasian students make up 41.2 percent of the county schools student population, but 79 percent of those suspended in the school year were black and Latino students.[50]

During a parent meeting I attended with more than fifty others, one parent expressed her frustration that her son had been kicked out of school. She said her son had been throwing paper at another student along with two others, and she took issue with the fact that he was the only student singled out for suspension. Even though the room was very diverse, several black and Hispanic parents shared the same frustration regarding their sons: certain groups were punished at rates significantly higher than others. Unfortunately, these incidents do in fact take place, because in many of the middle- and upper-class families, which is the socio-economic background of many of the teachers making these decisions, the expectation and level of accountability is different.

When young men are able to develop healthy, encouraging relationships with their teachers, they will be better understood academically. However, this rapport can only be built through interaction and genuine concern, which many teachers don't have for young men, or aren't sure how to express. The message several young men hear from school when expelled is that the teacher and educational system don't care. Once a feeling of abandonment sets in, the young men return to school harboring an attitude of resentment and bitterness. Suspension ignores the underlying issue and is a root cause of the disproportionate number of black, Latino, and Hispanic males in juvenile detention centers and prisons across the country. A 1997 survey by the Dyslexia Foundation found that about 70 percent of boys in juvenile institutions suffer from learning disabilities. Approximately 80 to 90 percent of all convicted felons are high school dropouts.[17]

When our young men are suffering from learning disabilities and a lack of healthy ways to express themselves, suspension isn't the answer. The only real benefit of this pseudo-solution is that the teacher and school are relieved of dealing with the so-called at risk young men. In some instances, students consider expulsion a treat, and occasionally they influence others to join them.

If the cycle of school violence and increasing dropout rates among boys is ever going to stop, our educational system must look for ways to help these young men, instead of ignoring the problem. The viable solution is to create a diversionary program that assists young men in dealing with the underlying issue that provoked the initial behavior.

Diversionary programs can serve as the vessel that channels negative energy in the proper direction. Essentially, negative behaviors all come down to BS, which stands for belief systems. Diversionary programs deal with the belief system and how it was created and focus on reprogramming it. Such programs creatively get young people to question their own behaviors and provide alternative options in dealing with them. This is a critical concept that I train adults on in my workshop called "Winning Back Our Boys: The Ultimate Gameplan for Parents and Teachers," because it's the driving force behind every human action.

Boys with behavioral problems usually are sent to programs that have untrained and underpaid staff. And these people are attempting to assist the young men? These "high-risk students" then receive the least preparation and care and the lowest expectations of all other groups of students. This further proves the negative perception that many of the young men have about society—"It doesn't love me," "It doesn't support me," and "I have no place within it"—igniting the already intense anger and pain they hold inside.

How can a society that pretends to be child centered justify culturally approved neglect? As a society, we have to take a closer look at the school system, because it's where children spend the most time. If we're honestly seeking the best interest of the students, let's place the more experienced teachers and the best resources in the more deprived areas with the students who need them the most. Doing so will create a more balanced educational field, while sharing vital resources that many have been deprived access to. Keep in mind, this isn't an attempt to bring the strongest students down to be equivalent with the weakest; rather, we should seek to raise the weakest up so they, too, can have a chance at achieving success.

School failure is often blamed on more obvious causes like low pay, teachers, parents, and students, and some of this blame is legitimate. However, today's procedures and guidelines are often enforced by administrative staff that have minimal experience in the classroom and little understanding of what it takes for students to succeed. This makes it difficult for the teachers on the frontlines, who have to exercise certain plans that they know won't work. Consider this: Most high school curriculums shape students to be good employees instead of good employers. This is why most students choose employment over entrepreneurship. Students even begin to lose interest in school because their dreams aren't being nurtured. Most teachers and other adults in the educational system teach students how to rent a lifestyle instead of own one.

This is accomplished in a way most students are unaware of. Children are separated in school by a system called "tracking." Placing students in color groups, number groups, and even animal groups is a form of tracking. I once visited an elementary school where students were placed in "eagle" groups and "pigeon" groups. Understanding the nature of these two birds, which bird would you rather be? This system distinguished the students based on their ability to perform certain tasks. It's understood that the economy doesn't need every student to be a college graduate; it needs winners and losers, and this is what school systems produce. The workforce needs executives as well as janitors. While there is nothing wrong with being a janitor, most people in this profession never chose it as a first option. Unfortunately, in low-income areas, good behavior is valued over learning, which places many young people at the bottom of the tracking system. This is often due to the lack of preparation teachers are given to deal with issues that come up in low-income areas. Feeling insecure and ineffective, teachers are often relieved when students simply don't cause trouble that day. So students are praised just for doing what should be expected rather than for their academic performance.

Another major concern that must be taken into consideration as a result of the failure among young men is the effect of interaction with female teachers on male students. How women feel about themselves, their fathers, boyfriends, or husbands could all be factors influencing the way they deal with male students. Please keep an open mind on this subject.

At times, if we're having problems with a specific person from a distinct group, we may unconsciously direct our feelings at others whom we perceive to be a part of that same group. One colleague of mine came to work one day with a very unusual attitude. In a playful yet serious tone, she stated that she was "mad at all guys." It was obvious there was a conflict of some sort with her boyfriend, but what was most interesting was, by the end of the day, she had sent two students to the office. Both of them were male. I'm not insinuating this type of activity takes place often, but because young men misbehave disproportionately more than young women, it should be considered. It has been shown that boys in grades 4 through 8 are twice as likely as girls to be held back a grade and the rates are higher for boys of color.[39] Pair this with unequal treatment, and you'll find that in many instances boys act out as an expression of their desire to get expelled from school because they don't feel confident in their academic achievements. Boys cause about 90 percent of the discipline problems and constitute nearly 80 percent of the dropouts.[21] Young boys see school as a place of assimilation, not affirmation, and are gaining the title of being the new underclass.

When young men are placed with stern, caring male teachers, their outcomes are dramatically different. I have seen firsthand how the presence of a male figure in school environments improves the behavior, as well as the academic performance, of male students, especially black and Hispanic students. African American male teachers make up 2 percent of the educational community.[12] This doesn't give young black men many avenues to connect with someone they can physically or culturally identify with. Often, black males as well as other minority male students get discouraged and drop out when they don't see a positive, authoritative face that reflects theirs. The frustrations they express sometimes raises fear in teachers who have to deal with them. It's often unclear to teachers what they should do to address these issues.

In several instances, teachers don't understand the student's behavior or what triggered it, so the steps they take to address the behavior are perceived by the student as disrespectful. Regardless of race, the most effective way teachers can reach out to students is by expressing that their primary concern is about the student as an individual and not just an issue. However, many teachers miss the opportunity to focus on the individual, and as a result, it becomes difficult, if not impossible, to teach a child who, the teacher fears, doesn't understand, and who perceives the teacher as disrespectful. When a student feels to the slightest degree that the teacher fears him, the negative power he has over that teacher tremendously increases, allowing him the opportunity to challenge the teacher further.

During the first month of my teaching career, I was challenged by a student greatly feared by teachers in that particular school. I knew if I didn't set the tone at the start of the school year, he definitely would. After lunch one day, he came to class late, walked in the back of the room, spat out the window, and gave me a look almost as if he dared me to say a single word to him. I told him to close the window and get out in the hallway. He slammed the window and walked out of the classroom, muttering something under his breath. As I walked behind him into the hallway, I knew I had one shot and one shot only to take control of my class for the rest of the year. The class was going to follow either his direction or mine. When we were both in the hallway, I closed the door just enough to make him feel that it was just me and him, but I left it open enough so the class could hear what I was about to say. I had to let them know more than anything that I was not only in charge, but also that this was my class. Looking him dead in his eyes as my heart beat with anger, frustration, and uncertainty, I told him that he had better not ever disrespect my class again.

Raising my voice just enough so the class could hear me, but keeping it low enough that he didn't feel threatened, I let him know that I poured my soul into every student and respected everyone in the class as young adults and that if he wanted respect he had to give it. He looked me in my eyes for about four seconds, which seemed like eternity, only to realize that I wasn't going to lose the battle that he had been used to winning with so many other teachers. The passion and intensity I communicated at that moment not only demanded respect from him, but also from my entire class, because for the first time they heard a teacher put this student in his place. That incident spread around the whole school like wildfire. It communicated to every current and future student that Mr. Cannon really cared about his students, but he didn't play.

The challenge among males in school is not solely to undermine the teacher, but to boost their ego and confidence. They usually manipulate the environment in any way they can to display their strength. This behavior threatens many female teachers because, in many cases, the teacher's physical strength is no match for their male student. Most teachers never realize that the passion and genuine concern they show for their students will break down any possible barrier, even physical strength.

I'm well aware from my own experience that most teachers aren't trained or equipped to deal with young men who physically or verbally act out. This makes the suggestion to place them in special education more attractive to teachers, in order to avoid future conflict. However, young men displaying problem behavior desire love and correction, but too often adults assume the worst in them, dismissing the opportunity for positive change. The way young boys are wired, they need clear behavioral limits, one-on-one time with the opportunity to verbally express themselves, frequent changes in action, and the chance to physically express themselves and burn off energy. They also need other means to express outwardly what they feel inwardly, when the environment allows it.

I understand that teachers have a very difficult task. They are expected to keep many students quiet for an extended period of time, in one area, without any disruptions. A further challenge occurs when students are expected to learn what someone else decided was important for them, in a way that is not conducive to their style of learning. However, I'm not suggesting that we entirely revamp what's being taught, but rather that we take into consideration what could be more effective for the student.

If we pay attention and observe children, they will teach us how to teach them. Unfortunately, too many teachers overlook this opportunity because they choose not to see anything beyond their own scope of experience. This is where conflict can occur between the student and teacher. For example, many teachers who grew up in middle- or upper-class homes expect their students to have the same resources they or their children had at that age, such as globes, computers, and reference materials. It's unfair to assign certain homework assignments that require specific resources and materials that some families don't have and can't afford. This punishes those without financial means and rewards the privileged with extra credit or better grades. Teachers have been known to give extra credit for assignments that include the use of special graphics. Doing so does not evaluate the child's learning, but rather gives credit to the household assets they possess. Students should neither gain nor lose points based on their parents' assets.

Another factor that strongly influences behavior is the students' home environment. A student who is viewed as a troublemaker and is written off as such may actually be a great student with vast potential that will never be nurtured by those with the opportunity to do so. Students sometimes come to school hungry, abused, neglected, and even abandoned, but teachers and administrators often overlook these issues. Children who are labeled ADD often suffer from nutritional deficiencies, not any kind of attention deficit disorder. If their diets improved, the rate of ADD placement would decrease dramatically.

Regrettably, some teachers who are aware of their students' unfortunate situations offer minimal solutions. They may even tell students the way to help change the situation at home is by changing their behavior at school. Such suggestions further feed the students' belief that the teachers don't understand. Asking young people to just change their behavior by themselves, in light of their home situation, is like asking a fish in the ocean to clean its own water. After countless failed attempts to get assistance, young men sometimes cry out for more help by getting into more trouble. A young man may feel the more attention he brings to himself, whether positive or negative, the greater possibility he'll receive help. These students' mindset becomes that they receive attention only when they get into trouble.

In most cases, the way teachers respond to these young men makes or breaks their educational success. Students initially perceive teachers as being the experts in everything because of their position, and their words sometime override what parents say at home. Therefore, if students feel their teachers won't help and support them, it's a significant blow to their drive to learn. Teachers who don't support or genuinely encourage their students often share their feelings with colleagues who have those same feelings about their students. The conversation within the teachers' lounge can be extremely negative, offering little but skepticism for a particular student's ability to improve.

Behind closed doors is where you find some teachers who discredit and degrade the same students they are supposed to be teaching, helping, and encouraging. In this setting, teachers often justify to each other why their students are failing, rarely considering that it could be something they're doing. This makes matters worse for the students, because their instructors are convinced that the problem lies solely outside their teaching parameters.

A teacher at the school where I taught always complained about his students and their lack of focus. Sadly enough, the administration and other teachers knew it wasn't the students. The problem was his vast knowledge and lack of skill in simplifying it so his students could understand. He was so smart that he assumed everyone knew what he knew, and because of this, he wasn't able to connect or communicate with the students so they could understand his teaching. As a teacher, I felt compelled to support my colleague, but not at the expense of several students getting their educational needs met. Many teachers are like my colleague, and unfortunately, their tenure protects them, as do their personal relationships with the same administration that can't see that their job is considering what's best for the students, not protecting the feelings of their friends.

Another contributing factor regarding young boys' behavior is that schools place more emphasis on sports than academics. If the football team or boys' basketball teams are participating in any kind of championship, the school will have a pep rally or assembly in appreciation of how they're representing the school. If they win, they're given large trophies or medals and are placed, literally or figuratively, on pedestals and praised for their athletic ability. If you took any one of these same young men and disconnected him from sports—placed him on a champion science, art, drama, chess, debate, reading, or any other academic club, for instance—the response from the student body, teachers, and administrators would be completely different. For excelling in one of these academic areas, a student is more likely to receive a certificate of some sort and a small button, in front of a very small audience consisting mainly of parents, other student participants, and the few teachers who were part of the club.

When more emphasis is placed on athletics than academics, athletes begin to feel as though they're so important on the field or court that their behavior elsewhere doesn't matter. As an elite athlete myself in high school, I noticed certain teachers gave very little, if any, homework on game days. Several guys on the team would show up late for classes, including me, with little punishment, if any. Whenever I was faced with a teacher who didn't care that I was an athlete and intended to send me to the office for being late, I knew what other teachers would write me a hall pass to keep me out of trouble. In a sense, athletes understand that they are defining the school by the sport they represent and lose focus on what's really important, their education. If you think about it, you never hear about a school being known by the young men who participate in its debate club, but you always hear about schools known for boys' basketball or football teams. When young men recognize this, sports become the ultimate focus instead of academics. This is evident when young men are asked if they want to go to college. The overwhelming response is that they want to play in the NBA or NFL, never viewing college attendance from an academic perspective. Some of these responses come from young boys who've never played sports in their lives but desire the same treatment their jock classmates have received.

The value and expectation we place on the quality of education our young men receive will greatly impact our communities in the future. Proceeding with the path we're on, we can only expect further destruction. This has become evident even at the collegiate level. In 1999 in colleges across the United States, there were over 15,000 courses focusing on women's issues and needs, compared to less than 200 courses offered to their male counterparts.[17] However, this academic imbalance is overshadowed by male collegiate sports; media airwaves are saturated with stats and highlights from Saturday's games.

Academic expectations of young men must be raised on every level: both what schools expect from young men and what the young men expect from themselves. They must learn that sports can be the means to an academic end, but academics are not a means to a professional sports career. As a college football player, I saw how each year hundreds of young men dropped out of college when they weren't picked up in the NFL draft and their college football eligibility ran out. Staying in college to earn a degree was never in the plans because they had chosen classes that made it easier on their college football schedules, not classes that led to a career they were interested in. They were deceived into thinking that if they could just get to college, the next level of sports achievement was almost guaranteed. I witnessed from experience why this mindset was further supported on the college level, especially when students were instructed to miss class for practice or film sessions. It is not my intention to slander the integrity or reputation of university or college football programs. Rather, I wish to raise the level of academic expectations of our young men so they don't become a second-tier statistic—meaning they made it past the first hurdle, high school, but tripped and failed miserably, never crossing the finish line.

KEY POINTS FROM THIS CHAPTER

CHAPTER 2

THE BROKEN MALE

PUTTING THE EMOTIONAL PIECES BACK TOGETHER

CHAPTER 2

Young people today are under more pressure and stress than any other generation before them. Many of our youth have been driven over the edge by the negative impact of divorce, multiple relocations, multiple (or no) caretakers, media pressure, continuous exposure to violence, the increase of sexual abuse, and the absence of parental expectations. In conjunction, young boys are told repeatedly to "stop crying," "stop being a baby," "stop acting like a girl," and "wipe those tears away." They are told that "big boys don't cry." Statements like these have conditioned young men to suffer alone, in silence, without expressing emotions, so they won't be considered weak. This practice has led to generations of young boys harboring resentment as a result of unexpressed feelings. Everyone needs a way to positively express how they feel or they will act out, which in most cases is done in a negative way. All babies are born with an emotional clean slate. It isn't until they interact with others that their emotional states form. For some, their feelings and emotions are supported, while others are shushed or discouraged. Ignoring children's emotions and preventing them from expressing themselves has detrimental effects. Young boys are taught to deny emotions and rarely are encouraged to embrace them and utilize the vocabulary necessary to express themselves. No matter how many times we push certain feelings or emotions under the rug, they still exist.

It's human nature to crave what we don't have. Think about the child who lives with one parent who cooks, cleans, and cares for him or her with no assistance from the other parent. In most cases, this child longs for the attention of the missing parent. Oftentimes, children in such a situation will act out in negative ways to try to fill this void. The same holds true for young people who just want to be heard and given the chance to be vulnerable and express their emotions, frustration, or experiences. When they are constantly ignored, not given the opportunity to express themselves, it's like a pressure cooker with no release valve; it will eventually explode. The people who do explode often release their built-up hurt and denial through self-inflicted pain and self-hatred. This occurs in the form of self-mutilation such as cutting, piercing, poking, and pulling. When this doesn't soothe their rage, they direct anger outward, inflicting pain on others, often escalating in scale over the years to culminate in violent crime such as homicide.

Young people who are abused often cry out for help. Sometimes, they verbalize their pain to others by saying what they're going to do to themselves or others, hoping that someone intervenes before they act. All people expressing the desire to harm themselves or others should always be taken seriously. Even if violence is not in their character, the fact that they've verbalized it places pressure on them, and they may feel obligated to act on their words.

Whites, blacks, Latinos, Asians, Hispanics, and other ethnic groups all handle emotional issues differently. Whites and Asians tend to internalize their rage and may shoot, stab, cut, and kill themselves. White males account for the majority of youth suicide deaths, at almost 60 percent.[44] Suicide is the third leading cause of death among youth ages ten to nineteen. In the United States alone, 1,921 young people in this age group took their own lives in 2000.[3] In America, a person dies by suicide every eighteen minutes, and it's estimated that there are twenty suicide attempts for every successful youth suicide.[49] In contrast to whites and Asians, blacks, Latinos, Hispanics, and other minorities tend to externalize their rage and may shoot, stab, cut, and kill others. In the United States, approximately 2,500 black youth (aged fifteen to twenty-four) die annually from gun homicide, along with 950 Hispanic youth.[51]

Cultural differences cause some of our youth to express their anger inwardly, while others turn their anger outward. Regardless of how it happens, death is always final. Suicide is a permanent solution to a temporary problem, whereas homicide is a permanent problem that comes in the form of a temporary solution: both result in a death that could have been prevented.

A few warning signs of suicide in youth range from talking of suicide directly, making drastic behavioral changes, taking extensive risks in various forms, giving away special possessions and making arrangements to take care of unfinished business, losing interest in usual activities, and showing signs of depression. Drastic decline in school performance, sleeping too much or too little, and losing interest in social and sports activities are signs of depression that could also lead to suicide. This is only a partial list, so if a child's behavior raises concerns, take the time to talk to the child to see if there are any problems. In most cases it's better not to overreact, but when suicide is suspected, it's better to be safe and possibly prevent a life from being taken. An adult can help support the child by listening to him and allowing him to express his feelings. Keep in mind, however, that criticism should be avoided at all costs, because many youth are ticking time bombs looking for any reason to explode.

Maintaining a line of communication with children gives them a much-needed outlet. This is crucial because so many children are searching for help and feel they have nowhere to turn. Many of the same signs that serve as warning signals of self-injury and suicide could also be red flags for potential violence against others, including homicide. Youth who are obsessed with guns, and who are unable to express their internal emotions, might also be of concern. In addition, children who have been picked on and made fun of and show signs of depression might also pose a threat of retaliating by plotting the death of their bullies. The warning signs of homicide are, in most cases, harder to detect than suicide. However, youth who display violent behavior and emotional abuse are often prime candidates for this type of explosive behavior and should be handled delicately.

These young men who display violent behavior, in nearly every situation are heavily guarded and feel as though the world is against them because of the experiences they've had with a few people. Unfortunately, the people who should have protected them have inflicted pain on them instead—their parents, family members, school systems, and even their churches. A young man I once mentored in Columbus, Ohio, opened up to me regarding why he had contemplated suicide. During his youth, until the age of seventeen, he was raped by four of his older brothers. He explained that he would run away from home often, for extended periods of time, because his mom didn't believe him when he would tell her what was happening. After countless attacks, he finally left for good as a way to escape the abuse.

On occasion, he would call and let me know how he was doing and give me his new contact information as well as updates about his life. I remember one conversation in particular, when I asked him how everything was going. Nothing could have prepared me for what was to come. After a brief pause, he said, "Well, I need money for my rent. I'm trying to graduate from high school, I'm hungry, and I just found out that I am HIV-positive." I was shocked, to say the least, because I knew he had contracted the virus from one of his older brothers, and there was no way of knowing which one.

This sexual abuse left him confused about his sexuality and his identity. It made him wonder about death coming sooner rather than later, and he felt alone because he had no organizations or support systems to help him address the issues he was facing.

When young men are sexually abused, they feel stigmatized, which in most cases is the most damaging aspect of their assault. The experience of sexual abuse causes many young men to try to prove their masculinity by becoming what's known as hyper-masculine. They attempt to compensate for their experience by having sex with multiple female partners or engaging in other dangerous behaviors to prove their masculinity. When an individual can't accept his body, for any reason, he loses vital honest contact with it and, in turn, loses vital contact with reality. His own body becomes objectified as a source of counterfeit identity.

Unfortunately, parents who have also suffered sexual abuse at an early age inadvertently pass on this type of behavior through the way they behave with or converse with their sons. Victims of abuse often victimize others in various forms. They may physically or mentally abuse others due to the rage that has built up within them as a result of their own abuse. The person who abused them could be deceased, incarcerated, or inaccessible, so they take out their hurt and anger on others who are just as vulnerable as they were when the abuse took place.

Young men are far less likely than young women to tell someone about their abuse, because it attacks the only strength they have, which is the false strength of masculinity. There may be several reasons for this, one being that society rarely offers a place for young men to go and be vulnerable about the subject of abuse. Most male victims who have been raped or molested believe that reporting such an incident makes them less of a man and could result in future retaliation from the aggressor. Girls are encouraged to report abuse as well as ask for help. Young men are taught to suppress their hurt and pain, therefore encouraging them to deny their issues. This message starts when boys are young adolescents.

In our society, traditional gender roles dictate that young men should have strength, self-reliance, and control. They can't be victims as well. This lack of recognition of victimhood makes it difficult for young men to get in touch with feelings of fear, hurt, and pain, rather than anger. Our culture doesn't permit vulnerability for men because it's perceived as weakness. As a young man, there is a certain safety in being angry. This type of thinking has conditioned young boys with low self-esteem to victimize themselves by denying their emotions. This sets them up to perpetuate the cycle of abuse they have experienced in their own lives, feeding into destructive behaviors that lead to negative reinforcement. Young boys who have experienced sexual abuse are often confused, questioning themselves about why others chose to victimize them. This confusion causes them to place a name and face to their issue before they attempt to deal with it.

Every year, millions of dollars are spent on assisting female victims of rape. However, young men who experience the same humiliating experience receive minimal if any attention at all. Few crisis centers or counselors are even trained to deal with this issue. Men who are incarcerated experience sexual assault at a much higher rate than do women, especially when children who are tried as adults and adults are locked up together. Such incidents are devastating, and many are not reported or given attention, even if authorities are aware they occurred. This can result in desperate measures by the victims, who sometimes attempt to kill themselves or the abuser. After being released back into society without any assistance, these same victims are more likely to turn their suppressed anger toward others.

Abuse is not limited to sex. Many young men are psychologically abused when they are verbally exploited as a means of motivation. This is often demonstrated in athletics, where a coach might yell or curse at the players as a way to "inspire" them. Oftentimes the goal is accomplished, but not without embarrassing and emotionally damaging the young men.

Similar damage can be done to youth when their parents don't accept them for who they are and constantly encourage them to be more like their siblings or friends. Some young boys have been torn down so much that they develop an inner abuser. The inner abuser is a voice from within that calls them stupid or incapable of doing anything right. Comparing children to one another always leaves the least of them feeling abandoned or inadequate. "Children that are abandoned by family as well as society make up the highest number of homeless people, unemployed, and prison population as adults."[17]

Most of these at-risk young boys come from single-parent homes where the stress level is high because the mother is faced with the responsibility of caring for the child or children alone. This all-too-common situation leaves many young boys emotionally and sometimes even physically abused as the mother has no other relief for her own anger and stress. These mothers may constantly remind their sons of how much they are like the fathers whom the sons have grown to resent. Boys who were abused by their mothers as youth have a higher predisposition for abusing their spouses as adults. Women who have been abused by their spouses are more likely to abuse their sons. This creates a vicious cycle of violence that never ends.

The relentless exposure to pain and violence may lead a child's brain system of stress hormones to become unresponsive. It just stops working, like a keypad that's been pushed too many times. Reaching this level is highly dangerous because the child then loses compassion for his life and the lives of others. He loses touch with emotions, develops a callous sense for pain, and views everyone outside of his shadow as a possible threat. These feelings that he loses touch with are necessary for his survival. When we have a physical problem, our body has an intelligence that responds so that our mind will take note of what's happening. When we ignore or deny the signals, it disrupts all of the interpersonal skills necessary for nurturing healthy relationships. We live by the philosophy that pain is weakness leaving the body. Before exposing our pain or weakness, we first build a wall. The wall is very difficult to get through or over, causing us to feel as if we're at war and have just crossed enemy lines.

Most of our youth are tough and callous due to their interpretation of social messages. The movies, music, video games, and adults in their lives all send social messages, and most of these messages are hurtful to our young people. As caring adults, we must understand that in the world of psychology, fear and pain are beneath all anger. The message children receive is that they have to be rich, successful, popular, well-liked, and accepted. When our youth fall into a constant battle to be approved of and accepted, the question they're asking with this behavior is, "Am I enough yet?"

Humans all operate with two levels of emotions: either survival-based emotions or opportunity-based emotions. Survival-based emotions are triggered when a person feels threatened, afraid, or fearful. Opportunity-based emotions are triggered when a person feels hopeful, excited, or stimulated. The false perceptions that boys often have cause them to operate from their survival-based emotions. Therefore, they become masters at hiding their emotions; they use humor, anger, or even unresponsiveness. The reason these negative habits persist is because they think they will derive some kind of benefit from them; otherwise, the habits would just go away. We have to help the boys analyze what they think this benefit will be. When they're able to look closely at what's happening, it will help them see there is no real payoff and then eliminate the survival-based emotions altogether.

Many youth use drugs and alcohol as a cover-up to give them the appearance of being happy, that life couldn't be better for them. They don't realize that nothing cuts off true happiness more than the false claim that it already exists, because you can't destroy a negative feeling you're not conscious of. Our young men must understand that when they expect something like a substance or someone who's not capable to take away their inner pain, it will never heal the underlying wound that's causing it. They are using these mechanisms as an attempt to self-medicate their pain and depression. This is their way of temporarily escaping from reality and vacationing from their problems. In the end, they always feel more pain, hurt, emptiness, and confusion. The core issue is that they feel as if they're not enough of something they think they should be. Therefore, they form a relationship with the substance, which helps them cope and perform in a way they lack the confidence to do when they're sober. It makes them feel complete, and they base their entire identity on how available the substance is to them.

Many young men are shut away in prisons, youth institutions, and special education classes because society has failed to find ways to address their needs. The highest degree of emotional abuse is neglect, which has become the normal expectation from adolescent boys. They've even grown to be skeptical about receiving help from police because they feel they're more likely to be arrested than assisted. Many times these are false perceptions they've developed from what they've heard, while other times it may be reality based on actual experience. From their perspective, they see helping law enforcement as a trap, having no possible way of escape.

I have spoken to several young men across the country who have grown hopeless and have given up on the possibility that life will get better for them. One in particular, a seventeen-year-old inmate in Lancaster, Ohio, said, "I have the school system against me, the prison system after me, and no family to support me, so what's the point?" However, as caring, responsible, loving adults, we should always be able to combat this question by pointing out that these young men have brought something to this world that wasn't here before. They are equipped with a talent, skill, or ability that millions are depending on, and they are the only ones who can activate it. It's imperative that we see in these young men more than they see in themselves. We must find ways to welcome all of their potential and creativity and assist them in honing their skills so they can become what they were created to be.

One of the best ways to be an asset to young people is by letting them know that we hear not only their words, but also their messages. When children act out, adults for the most part assume why they did it. In many cases, these assumptions are incorrect. Our opinions often determine their treatment and punishment. We might be surprised if we asked the children why they did what they did and really listened to their response. To effectively deal with youth, adults should never react; always respond. As much as possible, always stay even tempered; never display an emotion that could be perceived as negative. An adult's tone and physical expression determines the openness of that child. Always remember, ultimately, children want to satisfy adults and gain our approval, so they'll read nonverbal messages and respond according to what they feel we really want. Often, adults react and explode, which makes children shut down and feel it's better to simply listen rather than say what they really want and need to say. We need to teach our young people that their voice matters. When we continue to teach our children what we think, instead of how to think, we project our voice onto theirs and communicate that their voice has no meaning.

Whenever adults interact with a young person of any age, it is imperative that they remain conscious of the words they say around the child. Too often our words send negative messages to youth that impact how they feel about themselves and others throughout their entire lives. Examples of these harmful statements include, "You drive me crazy," "You make me sick," "You get on my nerves," "You gave me these gray hairs," and "You're going to drive me to drink." Have you ever said or heard statements like these? All of them send negative messages that make young people feel guilty, worthless, and even bitter.

Whenever I speak in detention centers, I always ask the young men how many have a dad at home. Close to 95 percent say they don't, so I ask them if they have a good relationship with their mothers, and most of them say no. When I ask why, the most common responses they give include, "She doesn't like me," "We don't get along," or "She always treats me like I did something to her." Then I ask them how many have ever heard this before: "You act just like your—" and they finish my sentence by saying "daddy/father." They understand that their father is viewed negatively, someone who makes their mother or other caregivers mad even when he isn't around, because he reminds them of something bad. In their minds, this is how the world sees them, too. Regardless of what their father has done, a child should never be charged with the same crimes. It's not the child's fault.

When we place labels or certain expectations on young boys, it's like handing them a script they feel they have to follow. "My son is just like his father, my oldest is my problem child, my youngest is the stubborn one of the bunch, the middle child is the angel, and my daughter is going to save us all." Whether the label is positive or negative, it's a lot of pressure to put on anybody, especially a child. How parents think of their children can be communicated in seconds, and when you multiply these seconds by the number of hours, days, and years children hear these messages, you realize how powerfully young people can be influenced by their parents' opinions of them. Not only are their feelings about themselves affected, but their behavior is as well.

Many times others place labels on children that are negative. When they aren't well equipped at home or don't have enough positive ammunition to pull from, there will be nothing in place to stop them from believing what others say. So many young people today are living the opinions of others, which are destroying them because they have nothing in place to combat it.

In essence, we have to encourage the use of emotional vocabulary among boys. We should allow them the opportunity to express their emotions without being criticized or feel their identity is being attacked for doing what many perceive as weak or feminine. Boys need to know that expressing their emotions is normal and natural and that these emotions serve as a smoke alarm. Imagine the primary function of a home's smoke alarm: it warns that danger is present and that help is needed. If a fire took place and there was no smoke alarm, someone could easily be seriously injured or die. We have to be the smoke alarm in the lives of young people, detecting a possible fire before it turns into blazing flames. They need us to recognize the warning signs they give and assist in their rescue. The best defense against destructive forces is offensive teaching. Preventing the bad before it happens is always more effective than criticizing them after they've happened.

KEY POINTS FROM THIS CHAPTER

CHAPTER 3
SEXPLOITATION

THE DECEPTION OF MANHOOD AND WHAT HAS TO BE DONE TO STOP IT

CHAPTER 3

Sex is a controversial topic, in particular when adults attempt to discuss it in relation to young people. There are two schools of thought regarding sex and youth. One is that people who made mistakes in their youth believe that teens today will make the same mistakes they made. Many times, these adults don't give youth the benefit of the doubt or a chance to prove they can make better choices than previous generations.

At the other end of the spectrum, some adults who did not have sex until marriage have unrealistic expectations that today's teens will do the same. They have no concept of the challenges that our young people face today. Many of these adults hide behind a perfect image that doesn't exist and blindly believe that young people will do so as well. In the same manner that the "Just say no" drug slogan didn't work in the 1980s, telling young people to "just wait" to have sex is equally ineffective. The purpose of this chapter is to momentarily put aside both views, dig deep, and look at the root cause of why young boys in particular resort to sex.

Most people believe the most important male sex organ lies behind the zipper. True, that's of utmost importance, but the primary sex organ for young boys is their brain. Doctors, sex therapists, parole officers, counselors, and anyone else who deals with this subject will all tell you that the brain is the largest sexual organ humans have. However, when adults attempt to address the issue of sex either indirectly or directly, the brain is rarely accounted for or even mentioned. Countless studies support the fact that even after age twenty-one, the brain is still developing. Businesses understand this, which is why, for instance, rental car companies require drivers to be at least twenty-five years of age before they can rent a car. When the brain is disassociated from sexual activity, the spiritual, psychological, and neurological aspects of sex are also ignored. For example, if a young man comes from a home where he never received intimacy, he may feel emotionally deprived, and his way of filling this emotional gap could be to act out sexually.

While acting out sexually, he's also sending his brain negative messages about sex, which conditions him to think about sex in ways that are very unhealthy. During this process, the brain is trained to accept a neurological reality that soothes the emotional neglect. From a neurological perspective, the brain adopts this method of getting its needs met. Young people who adopt this type of programming reinforce it by acting out sexually, reinforcing the thought that sex medicates their inner being. The brain becomes incapable of distinguishing if this method is appropriate or inappropriate. In most cases, the only way to correct this behavior is to create new pathways and retrain the brain so it becomes a partner in this process rather than an enemy.

Young boys resort to this type of thought process to deal with issues they struggle with emotionally. To avoid dealing with the current or past trauma in their lives, sex becomes the emotional aspirin that deadens their internal pain. It is normal today for children to be raised in single-parent situations, and in an ever-alarming trend, many children have been abandoned by their parents. The absence of one or both parents, due to death, divorce, or neglect, is very painful and confusing for a young person. Both parents are important in the lives of all children because they both serve to meet specific needs. When children grow up in an environment without parents, they lack the feeling of emotional safety and oftentimes act out compulsively in search of security. This isn't just limited to sexual behaviors; drugs and alcohol abuse are byproducts as well. Sex, however, serves as the first medication to numb the pain of abandonment.

Dr. Douglas Weiss, a noted expert on sexual addiction, compares human needs to a sponge that needs watering on a daily basis. In this analogy, the sponge would be the individual's personality, how he feels about himself overall as a person. The continuous moisture this sponge needs is praise, encouragement, positive affirmation, as well as approval. Young people who have grown up in dysfunctional families can quickly attest that their sponge is in desperate need of water, because they didn't know where or how to ask for help. This emotional deprivation causes them to live with an internal ache that continues to produce agonizing pain until the issue of their emotional neglect is dealt with properly. Unfortunately, many of these young people turn to sex to fill the void.

Adults who aren't willing to think in realistic terms about young boys and sex are only prolonging this pain. It isn't until the root cause is discovered and dealt with that a viable solution is found. While things such as condoms may protect from physical consequences of sex such as unwanted pregnancy and sexual diseases, they can't protect young boys from the psychological damage of sex, which can last a lifetime.

To provide a more balanced view of sex, let's look at another perspective that's often ignored. During the imprint period, which is between the ages of birth to six years old, the human mind seeks meaning. This is the primary reason why children want to know what everything means and how and why it operates the way it does. Take a look, for instance, at little children's conversation; they're full of questions that start with "why." "Why can't I have that," "Why do you have to go to work," "Why can't I stay up late," and the list continues. After a while, adults lose patience, get irritated, don't have the answer, or don't want to address certain issues. The adults tell them to stop asking questions, which is very detrimental because children eventually shut down and stop seeking meaning. They stop trying to figure things out, which is actually healthy for them. Many of these issues that adults want to ignore really need to be addressed because they're important to the children, who are desperately seeking answers.

Adults often shut children down by saying "because I said so," "because I'm the grown-up," or "because I'm the parent," which communicates that asking questions is wrong. Children often live with this conclusion for the rest of their lives. When I worked as a schoolteacher, countless times I witnessed young people's hesitation to ask questions because of early programming from their parents. Their parents have told them, "Don't question my authority, do this because I said so, do that because I'm the parent." In reality, those are not quality answers for the children asking the questions. They're usually easy answers to allow the parents to escape a situation. These phrases offer nothing digestible to the child seeking answers to specific questions.

Very little can be explained by someone hearing an answer such as "because I'm the parent." This phrase makes no sense at all to the conscious mind of a child. It doesn't provide a tangible reason. Adults who grew up this way, programmed to think that certain rules should be followed simply because adults have power and authority, can relate to this. Young people should always respect authority, but should also be given answers to questions that are meaningful to their lives. It's detrimental to teach a child that asking questions is wrong, because the unconscious mind is wired to seek a meaning for everything. Humans are always trying to figure things out.

Not every new experience has a meaning, so we attempt to find one, even if it is not a true reflection of that experience. Each initial meaning is a decision of possible truth, and our interpretation determines that truth. For example, if a young person is abused, he may decide that it means certain things about himself, for instance that he is unlovable, ugly, or weak. Thus, his perspective is skewed.

In essence, when we experience an event, we must guess what it means because we have never experienced it before. We might not be convinced that our assumed meaning is the truth, but we have a hypothesis or theory about it. In all cases, the meaning that we create is designed to keep us emotionally safe. The unconscious mind's top priority is to keep us emotionally safe. Once we've made a decision that something is true, we start collecting emotional evidence to support it, because human beings like to be right. We either collect a lot of evidence over time, or something huge happens on an emotional level that gives us enough evidence all at once.

When we get enough evidence, our decision turns into a belief, and once it's a belief it begins to control our behavior. So once we think a certain way, we'll begin to behave that way and create experiences to match our beliefs. This has a direct connection with sex, because when young adults are given limited or no information about sex, they begin to create it themselves. They place their own meanings and interpretations on things, which are, in most cases, totally incorrect. This is why parents should never answer a child's question with "because I'm the adult" or "because I'm a grownup." By the age of fourteen or so, these same youth feel that they're grown, but their "adult" lives are based on just a few experiences. Maybe they have a job and have been told that adults have jobs or adults pay their own bills. They use this to justify why they should be able to do certain things. Parents might allow their child to have a job to pay his own cell phone bill, which hardly legitimizes him as an adult, but gives him a good enough reason to think he can do what adults do.

Adults must keep in mind that every action young adults take is asking some kind of question. When teens get jobs, they want to know if they can buy what they want now. When they get a job and buy what they want, many wonder, am I an adult now? More significantly, when young people have sex, in many cases this single act is asking a multitude of questions. This action asks, am I an adult now? Am I a man now? Is this going to make me feel better? Am I significant or important to somebody now? Will this get me the love that I'm searching for? Will this give me the validation that my father never gave me? Will this give me the attention that I want? Will this gain me acceptance and respect from my peers? Will this remove the insecurities I have? If I give this away, will it free me from the pain of when it was taken away from me by force?

In essence, adults tell teens not to have sex until they get married, so they'll stay healthy, so they won't get STDs or become teen parents, but most youth still desire more reasons why they shouldn't have sex right now. The reason is because the issues adults talk about are based on their past and personal experience, whereas young people aren't really thinking about these issues because they haven't had certain experiences yet.

These issues won't become relevant to young adults until they find out they're going to be parents or get an STD. In order for youth to focus on anything long-term, adults must address what affects them now. Youth couldn't care less about health, pregnancy, or STDs. They are concerned with being emotionally safe, being popular, being loved, being respected, becoming an adult, getting approval, escaping pain, and being validated. When these issues are addressed and tied to a long-term objective, young people can see the value of why it's now important for them to implement change in their lives.

In our culture, sex plays a key role in our perceptions, situations, activities, and many other aspects that impact our daily living. It's all over billboards, print media, and all forms of music, and is a part of almost every TV channel known to man. The image of sex painted in the media is false. It doesn't demonstrate the beauty of sex. Its true essence has been perverted. Today, people are looking for sex without love, love without marriage, and marriage without responsibility. Many people are having a lot more sex than true love in their relationships. These are all examples from which our young men learn unless they have someone in their lives modeling what they need to see.

Due to the lack of appropriate role models in young men's lives, they think they need sex in order to have a commitment in their dating relationships, when actually the proper way is to make a commitment and then celebrate it with sex. Our young people are experiencing sexuality in a casual and detrimental manner. Today's attitude is, have sex with whomever you want, and if you can't be with the one you want, enjoy the one you're with. Relationships like that always end up in pain and suffering, because one or both partners end up feeling deceived. When two people are enjoying the benefits of marriage without the commitment, their relationship is built on a fallacy. This is especially true when everything they're searching for in relationships can only be obtained through a healthy marriage. Youth aren't receiving the blessing of marriage but oftentimes experience the consequences of divorce. Their entire relationship is based on the amount of physical involvement they have with each other. When this element is removed from their relationship, the very basis of its foundation is diminished.

Many adults wonder if they are able to assist this new generation of young people with decision-making about sex. The question is not if we can help them make a decision, but what decision are we going to help our youth make. Even when we do not verbalize our assistance, we aid them in decision-making by the actions they see in us as their caregivers. We have a habit of allowing the media, society, and their so-called friends to make decisions about sex for them. Instead, they should be learning from loving, caring, and responsible adults who will help guide them through this journey. At some point, we have to ask ourselves why we are putting their dreams, goals, and lives in the hands of others who have no concern for their best interest. When adults don't share the proper information about sex with youth, it always leads to destruction. Some leaders take on the role of avoidance, while others are ashamed of what they've done and perceive educating youth about these matters as being hypocritical. If we sit back and just talk about how bad the situations are, they'll only get worse. However, if we make a conscious effort to be active in their solution process, they're certain to improve.

Our young men have virtually no correct information about sexuality. They use it to incorrectly address many of the needs and desires that are beyond just the feeling of sex. Some young men use sex as a way to gain the approval of their peers. When they have sex, one of the first things they do is tell their friends. It's almost meaningless if they can't verbally share their experience with others. This is a primary way for them to obtain respect from their male peers, especially when their father is not present to give approval on a regular basis. Sex has become the substitute for validation from fathers who aren't in the picture.

Young men might also have sex to feel a sense of accomplishment, as a way of challenging themselves and achieving positive reinforcement. The fact that sex is the only thing they feel they can be good at is the primary reason they use it in this manner. Many are told that they have failed at everything else in life, and this is the one tool they can use to feel successful. Most have been programmed to think that in order to be masculine, they have to deal with everything themselves. Sex is one of the most common mechanisms boys use to deal with issues they're going through.

After I spoke at a detention center about sex and the definition of manhood, a fifteen-year-old boy came up to me and thanked me for sharing. He went on to tell me that he had failed in sports and at school, and even within his family, but sex was the one thing he excelled at and gave him the type of attention that made him feel good about himself. His comments ripped through my heart; I found it sad that our young people have to turn to sex to get positive attention. In fact, it's a very irresponsible way to view and utilize sex. It's alarming to know that many of our young men come from settings where they have been allowed or even encouraged to be irresponsible in this manner. If you think about it, you can't be an irresponsible young man unless you were allowed to be an irresponsible boy. If they were allowed to be irresponsible at home with morals, values, responsibilities, and everything else, why wouldn't they be irresponsible with sex?

The example of the young man above relates to people using sex to fill a certain void in their lives. Many aren't aware of the underlying reasoning for their actions. They're creating patterns in their lives that will eventually lead to destruction. Most of the females these young men attract have never received proper attention from their fathers and are willing to give themselves to any male who might give them attention. They're seeking out father figures in young men who haven't yet discovered the solution to the same issues they're facing.

Even though these young women initially receive what they think they want, they're getting something totally different. Guys use love to get sex, and girls use sex to get love. A guy looking for his manhood through sex will tell a female whatever she wants to hear to get sex. He'll even change who he is to impress her as a way to accomplish his overall objective. The desperation in his quest to find his male identity will cause him to go to great extremes to find it, even if it means deception. When he finally discovers that she doesn't have what he's looking for, he will abandon her emotionally and physically. He might challenge her to see how much emotional damage he can inflict before she gives up on the relationship. Whenever she does, he then tests how much control he has over her to see if she will accept him back. If she does, he then uses sex to deceive her further, while deceiving himself in the process. In general, individuals locked in this cycle have sex just so someone will consistently give them positive reinforcement. The offer of minimal pleasure for a short time is enough to make them jeopardize all of their talents, skills, and abilities.

The act these young people are performing is an attempt to receive intimacy, which they believe is sex. Intimacy is the ability to share your true self, all of your fears, dreams, goals, and desires, even when you think others might not agree. The reality is, most young men and women can't be intimate with themselves or others because they don't know who they are; they are focused on being what they think others want them to be or who they feel they need to be around others. Thus, they hide behind sex to cover up their insecurities. Due to the lack of support and proper rearing, many of these young men are weak in their minds, weak in their responsibilities, and weak in their hearts. This explains why much of their focus is on their physical appearance, to cover up their inner insecurities.

How young men engage in sex reflects how they learned about it. They've been taught to use it as a scapegoat for many of the issues in their lives that they've not dealt with. The bottom line is that when people frequently participate in something, they develop a capacity for it, and that capacity is only fulfilled when the desire for it is satisfied. The major problem in creating these desires is that the appetite for them increases with each use.

Young people who fall into this cycle open themselves up to endless negative possibilities. The risks of emotional and mental agony that lead to depression and sometimes suicidal thoughts never enter their minds. Even when these topics do surface, the only thought young people can possibly entertain is, "It won't happen to me." Young men with unfulfilled emotional voids due to the absence of their father are at the highest risk of becoming teen fathers. Seventy percent of teen fathers do not marry the mother of their child and aren't active in the child's life. This creates the same vicious cycle into which they were born, leaving their own child to grow up empty-hearted and searching for fulfillment through sex.[34]

Fifty percent of teenagers who are sexually active get pregnant in the first six months of adding sex to their relationship.[8] This puts them at great risk for living in poverty for the rest of their lives, because out-of-wedlock childbirth in the United States is the leading determining factor of poverty.[34] Teen fathers and even certain adult fathers need to see a good model of fatherhood before they can demonstrate it themselves for the true opportunity and responsibility it is. This is why the reality of sex should be observed from the best perspective before people engage in it. Those young adults who don't have this perspective and have never been exposed to it and who then become teen fathers still need to be encouraged and given the opportunity to become the greatest asset they can be in the life of the child and mother—which is, a great provider. They need a clear understanding of how important their role is and motivation to take on this responsibility that they've created.

Young men in our society always hear about the legal system that will come after them for running out on their babies, so they immediately feel like a fugitive. It's evident to them that there are more legal procedures to punish them for not being a responsible father than there are means of assistance to show them how to become one. Young men who are given educational, financial, and social opportunities, along with respect, have proven to commit themselves to becoming the best fathers they can be.

The solution that some youth counselors have suggested is increasing condom availability, not realizing you can't put a Band-Aid on a bullet wound—it's not a cure. Condom use is at an all-time high. But even with increasing condom usage, we still have seen an increase in pregnancy and STD rates, so clearly condoms are not the answer. There is a lesson to be learned from the sexual revolution of the 1960s: there is no such thing as casual sex; it has emotional consequences. We're still suffering the consequences from the attitudes and choices of the so called free love era, almost fifty years later. Sex has been devalued and ignored as a possible emotional trigger or signal that there are deeper issues. Some might argue it is different today than back then, but the only real difference is that young people today are at risk of contracting over twenty-five major sexually transmitted diseases, whereas the hippies started out with only three. Today, sex is a primary cause of depression among teenagers that frequently leads to suicide, which was practically unheard of before the sexual revolution mentally infiltrated the previous morals and values that existed. However, their attitudes and behaviors in the 1960s toward sex and free love wasn't so free because it's costing millions of young people their lives today. In reality, what the sexual revolution has now created is just an easy excuse, because it doesn't require integrity, morals, values, or self-control.

When someone says that sex is not a big deal or it's okay as a solution, he or she is communicating that young people are too irresponsible to have self-control and aren't trustworthy enough to make the best decision. One might argue that young people are going to have sex anyway. That's equivalent to saying most young men in lower income areas are going to join gangs and shoot each other. If we take the attitude that they're going to do it anyway, let's go to their neighborhoods and give them bulletproof vests so they can at least be safe while they're shooting at each other. Instead, we need to raise the standards for our young men and teach them about self-control instead of birth control. When we push condoms on our young men, we're encouraging risk reduction instead of risk elimination. What many adults fail to realize is that young men actually become angry when we don't place high standards on them.

Sex also involves many physical and emotional aspects that most people are unaware of. During sex there are several bonding mechanisms at work that connect people in unknown ways. When males have sex, a chemical called oxytocin is released in their brain that stores images, situations, and sounds of all the people they've been with. Just as a computer scans pictures into a file, young boys are capable of taking mental pictures of various people, scanning them, and placing them in the computer files in their mind to visit later when they fantasize. It's like having a mental library that stores what people look like, smell like, and even act like during a sexual encounter.

Males are stimulated visually; they're attracted to the things they see. For this reason, young men are not as attached as females after sex, because they bond more with images than with an actual person. After sex, a man can just get up and leave because he doesn't physically need the woman anymore; he has the images to take with him. This is a prime example of why teenage boys grow up and have problems in their relationships—because of all the past images they've stored in their brains. This can be very painful for a young woman, because she doesn't understand what she did wrong and can't figure out why her boyfriend no longer desires her as he did initially. I've spoken with young men who have even admitted to taking images of different people and compiling them in their mind to form the ultimate perfect image.

This causes the young man to bond to a false image, which creates problems in his relationships with real people. No real person can compete with the false image he has created in his mind. This is because the images don't argue, they don't cry, they're always available, and they do whatever he tells them to do, which allows him to temporarily feel great about himself through self-deception. In these fantasies, young men become all-powerful, all-knowing, in control, loved, and cared for. This is why pornography is so dangerous; it distorts natural desires into a selfish lust for personal gratification. The bottom line is whatever people create a mental capacity for, their bodies respond to physically and treat as reality.

Young men are often frustrated with girls who wear provocative clothes because they feel the girls are teasing them. The question then becomes, what is provocative? To a degree, provocative could change with every situation. However, when a young woman exposes her body in such a way that leaves little to the imagination, young men have little respect for them. In young men's minds, what a young woman wears has a strong connection with what she might do sexually, which is not always true. So when young men perceive a young woman to be a certain way based on how she's dressed and it turns out that he's wrong, he will convince himself he's actually right. He'll justify to himself that if she didn't want to have sex or be treated a certain way, she wouldn't have dressed for the occasion. Remember, the conscious mind's job is always to seek emotional safety, even it if means deceiving it into believe something false is true. Frustration grows rapidly in these young men, because they're used to getting what they want and having everything under their control, based on fantasized experiences with images.

Often, boundaries are crossed when a guy touches a girl inappropriately to test what "kind" of girl she is and how far she'll let him go. Young girls often approach me after my workshops when I talk about this aspect of young men. They all want to know the same thing: why can't they wear what they want to wear without guys looking at them like a piece of meat? The second question that usually follows every time is, why do guys think about sex all the time? I explain how guys are wired to be stimulated by what they see and how the chemical oxytocin plays an important role in this process. Most of the young women leave with a better understanding but still think it's unfair that they have to be punished because boys can't control themselves.

In essence, the best way for young men to learn how to treat females is for mothers to express the importance of respecting young girls and for fathers to model this behavior to mothers. I'm well aware that most youth don't grow up with both parents in the home, so the odds of this happening might be slim. However, the behavior can also be taught by showing boys the consequences of those who disrespect women by not honoring them. I often ask young males how they would feel if someone disrespected their mothers, grandmothers, or other females in their lives whom they care about. The answers vary: some young men want to fight or disrespect the person who disrespected their loved ones, or behave inappropriately. What I get them to understand is exactly how others feel about the daughters, granddaughters, and sisters of the young women they might be disrespecting. Many of them say they never thought about it like that, which is powerful because they can see how their behavior has a direct negative impact on an entire group of people based on their single act toward another person.

These young people need to be exposed to couples who respect each other and have the happiness that the average person desires from a romantic relationship. One single mother I met at a workshop shared that she teaches this concept to her son when they're out in public by pointing out the characteristics and actions of couples who fit this description. At every opportunity that presents itself, we must teach young boys the proper information about sex, relationships, and the way they should view, treat, and respect all women. We have to raise and set the standard regarding sex and not leave this responsibility up to media or adults who have no standards for our children. Allowing society and certain media to be the pioneers of educating our youth culture about the aspect of sex and its pleasure, as well as destruction, will further erode the future of this generation.

KEY POINTS FROM THIS CHAPTER

CHAPTER 4

STOP. LOOK. LISTEN.

WHAT BOYS WISH THEIR PARENTS KNEW ABOUT THEM

CHAPTER 4

The initial pathway to prison, drugs, gangs, and violence for young men starts at home. The environment children grow up in greatly determines their results in their adult lives. For instance, a young boy who grows up in a loving and nurturing home is more likely to become a productive member of society than is a boy who is surrounded by domestic, alcohol, and/or drug abuse. What these young men witness, whether it is food for the soul or seeds of destructive thinking, manifests into their adult lives.

As parents and caregivers, we have a responsibility to our children to give them every opportunity for success. To do this doesn't mean we have to have a lot of money. Emotional support, love, and genuine concern don't cost a penny. For us to set a good example and act as a good role model, we must do so in the initial stages of these boys' lives. The reality is children do what they see and not what they're told. They receive their expectations from their parents based on what they see them do. We've all heard the expression actions speak louder than words. If your words don't match your actions, which do you think your child is going to emulate? Boys often experience distortion when they hear something and interpret it totally differently from how it is intended.

Most parents don't understand that you teach what you know but reproduce what you are. A genuine change must occur from within if young men are ever going to experience positive influences from their parents. Unfortunately, many young men don't have good role models in their parents. When young men see integrity, honesty, and a strong work ethic in their parents, they have a strong foundational model for their futures. The behavior we as parents desire in our children shouldn't be any different from our own. When parents aren't respectful, loving, hardworking, and considerate, it's hard for their children to act in that manner.

As a parent, the real challenge is between what you have done and what you're capable of doing. Many have done little for their children, which in most instances is very obvious. Instead of cultivating their children, some parents have actually allowed the foundation of their family to erode away. This is a vicious cycle. In a family where there is little or no parental involvement, the children often experience emotional problems, and in more severe cases, their health suffers as well. The worse the child becomes, the less the parents are willing to deal with the situation.

On the other hand, parents who do invest in the lives of their children always reap the benefits of their labor. Stronger bonds, healthy relationships, and higher self-esteem result in positive parent-child interactions, which consequently enable the children to form healthy and productive relationships in their adult lives. A good portion of this can be attributed to the mutual respect between parents and children.

For us to truly respect our children, we must make every attempt to see the world from their point of view. The world today is much different than it was when we were children. Our children—young men in particular—experience much more difficult problems than children did in the past. For this reason, it's critical for adults to use their experience and wisdom to assist today's young men in making the best choices possible. Gaining an understanding about the challenges they face today helps us gain their trust and lead them down a path filled with good decisions.

Imagine that you and your child are both batteries. You both are in a flashlight, but one of you is turned the wrong way. The flashlight won't work. Now let's say you both are facing in the right direction, but one of you has very little juice or none at all. Two things could happen: one, the light could work for a short period of time by draining the fully charged battery, or two, it won't work at all. However, if both of you were brand-new out of the package, together you could be a force that shines bright in the world and into the dark situations others might be facing. This analogy reminds me of a quote I read years ago on the Internet: "It's better to build a child than to repair an adult." So often, parents don't invest the time early enough to turn their children around, and after a while, it literally drains them, if they really care for their child. If young adults aren't given the proper direction from their parents, they find any road to take them there. Loving parents always think about what their children need tomorrow and plan for it today.

Numerous studies show that parents are the number one influence in a child's life. Children want boundaries, guidelines, restrictions, and expectations to be placed on them. Young men actually need these limitations, but they first need someone who cares and nurtures them into accepting these responsibilities. If for any reason a boy doesn't or can't understand what's expected of him in a situation, he may become quiet and withdraw. It's the nature of youth to resist, but it's the responsibility of loving adults to give them something to resist against. When parents don't communicate standards to their children, it's interpreted as "you don't love me" or "you don't care." The worst perception a child can have is that his parents have given up on him.

Unfortunately, this is a very common fear for teenage boys. And so what do they do? They push their parents further away to see if their parents really have any control. They actually fear their parents not having control, so to get their attention, they might ignore them, and to draw them closer they sometimes push the parents away. In some cases, this kind of conflict is needed because it gives parents an opportunity to learn how their children see the world and what life issues concern them.

Young men I've spoken to in juvenile detention centers across the country always say they wouldn't be there if they had more discipline placed on them early in their lives. Respect, honesty, and discipline should all be instilled in young men at an early age. If not, a parent will suffer the consequences rather than enjoy the benefits of their son's actions in the future. For instance, if a mother told a young man to do something, realistically she can't make him do anything unless she physically forced him. The difference is the foundation of respect she invested behind those words that make them meaningful enough for that child to honor her request. According to several young men I've met in detention centers, boys feel neglected if firm guidelines and performance standards aren't placed on them. They have a sense of security knowing that an external source of final authority has control. If parents relax the guidelines, they will react by forcing parents to respond to their actions. The absence of these standards actually sets them up for failure because those who escape the temporary consequences of their actions believe there are none.

Parents often make the crucial mistake of trying to be their child's friend. Before a friendship can be established, parents need to set limits and discipline and make certain that their children respect them as parents. Parents who replace being firm with being "nice" experience their children making a mockery of their disciplinary efforts. When parents and caregivers discipline these young men, they actually provide them with a value system for their lives in the world. I'm not insinuating there should be anything approaching abuse, but parents should establish good, corrective measures from which their sons can learn. Sometimes children are punished rather than corrected. No value is added by punishing alone. Correction needs to be followed with an appropriate punishment to give it value, sense, and meaning. When young men aren't aware of the wrong in their actions, nothing prevents them from repeating them. The most effective method of correcting their actions is to punish wrongdoing in private and praise positive deeds in public. When boys are disciplined in public, they feel humiliated and view the correction as a threat and not a warning. Often, they interpret warnings as love but see threats as hate. They need to know and understand that they have someone who's going to help them get through life's challenges and make it to victory.

We must raise our young men in such a way that when adversity comes and tries to make them sit, they will stand; when it threatens to make them stand, they will stand out; when it torments them to stand out, they will be outstanding; and when it challenges them to be outstanding, they will become the standards for others to follow. In order for them to truly reach this level of success, they must be trained in such a way that even when they want to give up, their heart desires the freedom that manifests after they take the next step toward righteousness. The desire in front of them has to be greater than the pain behind them in order to move into greatness.

Parents and other adults are like potters, and the young people are like the clay. A parent's job is not just to raise productive, respectful, emotionally and physically healthy boys and girls, but also to develop great men and women. Before this can take place, a person must first understand what's needed to produce such results. It is difficult to help someone if their needs haven't been properly assessed. It's the time spent with them behind the scenes early in preparation that validates who and what they'll become in the future. Children are like mirrors, reflecting back what kind of parents or guardian they have. There has to be a certain level of adult or parental involvement in order for them to reach the level of fulfillment to which these young men strive.

Young people today often lack the relationships with their grandparents that once instilled respect, wisdom, and values in the character of youth in the past. Actually, the best place for young people to become educated is at the foot of a wise older person. Here, they will find a part of the identity that has been misplaced, ignored, and to some degree lost. They can also find out where they came from and become educated about the accomplishments and success of their heritage.

Children love to learn about their family and how their parents and grandparents grew up. It's a form of social studies with personal meaning attached. I was surprised the first time my son asked me to tell him a story about my childhood. After several stories, he looked out the window with a gaze and a sound of subtle amazement and said, "I never have to watch TV again. I can just sit and listen to you for entertainment." He was most intrigued because he learned that his father really did understand what it was like to be a young child. He taught me that the relationships that truly grow are those with vulnerability, where failures as well as victories are shared. Before I shared with him, I was somewhat reluctant because of what he might think. After that day, I've used my childhood stories and experiences to connect with my children on a much deeper level.

It's great for parents to spend time with their children by telling them stories and becoming more vulnerable around them, without losing credibility. When I catch my son doing something wrong, I often tell him a story about when I did the same thing as a child and how I thought I was going to get away with it. The fact that I've shared these stories with him helps him understand that I know what he's doing and why he's doing it. This has strengthened our relationship, and he often jokes with me about how I sound and look when I'm correcting him for something he's done. As a parent, it's a joy to relate to your children in a loving manner, and even though they don't like correction, they understand why it's necessary.

Sonya Carson was someone who mastered these strategies. She used the vulnerability of her own life to motivate, inspire, educate, and produce the type of children she desired to have. Explaining her lack of education to her children allowed them to see the importance of theirs. A single parent, she would take her two sons to the library each week and required them to read two books and do a report on them. Initially, this was a struggle, but it wasn't long before they began to read more than what was requested of them.[36] Although other children were glued to the television, she limited her children to three programs a week. They spent the rest of their time reading, studying, learning musical instruments, and playing outside. Most people have never heard of this lady, but her efforts and commitment to her children have impacted the world. Today, one of her sons is the director of pediatric neurosurgery at the John Hopkins Hospital in Baltimore, Maryland. He's a successful author and is considered one of the top brain surgeons in the world. The world knows him as Dr. Ben Carson.

Some parents don't expect the same type of academic excellence out of their sons as they do their daughters, thereby diminishing the internal fabric necessary for their success. Early parental teaching and expectations have a direct impact on the future habits of young men. Habits will determine a child's future; negative habits breed negative consequences, whereas positive habits create positive rewards. Unfortunately, nothing is a bigger waste than an unsuccessful young man with talent that has not been utilized. A large part of that can be attributed to the lack of standards or expectations placed on him by his parents.

I'm always conscious of making sure I hold my children to high standards, regardless of what they're doing. It's understood that I won't let them get away without doing their best. I constantly remind myself that my children are different from each other, but the same standards apply. As a parent I've learned that children don't do what you say; they do what you do. This has made me a better person, husband, and parent because my children hold me accountable, just as I do them. My children and I have an understanding that they can hold me accountable for doing the right things as long as they communicate their thoughts and ideas in a respectful manner. This has opened our lines of communication in ways we couldn't have imagined before we implemented this agreement. Our method of enacting agreements instead of rules has been very effective because our accountability is based on our agreements about what's best for our future goals. Partnering with your children as a parent to achieve their goals as well as your own brings an excitement to the home that is priceless.

Regardless of race, religion, socioeconomic status, or background, parents are only as happy as their saddest child. Families have achieved happiness in several different ways, financial gain being one of them. Parents sometimes get into the habit of distributing "guilt money" to their children as a way to compensate for the time they aren't spending with them. They try to buy love from their sons, not realizing that the greatest gift doesn't come from the store, it comes from the heart—the sacrificial gift of quality time. Young men view guilt money as a way for adults to ease their own conscience for not fulfilling their responsibilities. It's better to be a gift than to buy one. Parents need to start asking the question, "What is it that children desire that money can't buy?" The indisputable answer is time. The way young people spell love is not L-O-V-E, but T-I-M-E.

Youth who are labeled as having ADD might have an attention deficit disorder, but only in the sense that the disorder they suffer is the deficit of attention they receive from their parents. Many young men are being robbed of their childhood because they have been left alone to deal with adult situations. It's becoming more prevalent, especially when you hear children saying "remember way back when," before they comfortably reach double digits in age. This statement is a sign of what adults have exposed them to or protected them from and how it made them feel. Children that are abandoned by family as well as society make up the highest number of homeless people, unemployed, and prison population as adults.[13] This indicates we are in for even more problems as increasing numbers of children fall into the abandoned or neglected category. Approximately 80 percent of abuse to children comes from parents, and 58 percent of abuse or neglect of boys is done by females.[17] The increase of single-mother households is a threatening sign for our boys of the future.

Young men who are raised by single women frequently ask themselves, "Why do I have to be raised by a person who's mad at the man I look like?" Oftentimes these women see the image of their son's father in their son. This makes it extremely difficult for these mothers to withhold the anger they feel at the lack of support from their son's father. When a young man is constantly looked upon as the man of the house, in the absence of an actual man, he feels confused by the role forced upon him. Many times, mothers unconsciously look to their son for friendship and protection when these needs are not otherwise being fulfilled. When those expectations aren't met, they get frustrated with their son, never realizing that he's not equipped to take on that role. Once he sees himself as a protector of his mother, it distorts his view of her as an authority figure. That's why it's extremely important for fathers to be in their son's lives even if they aren't with the mother.

In general, mothers are more concerned with the safety, health, and emotional state of a child. In contrast, men are more concerned with discipline and the achievement of the child. Both concerns are important in the holistic approach to young men's development. The percentage of youth living in single-parent homes has more than tripled in the last three decades.[24] Ironically, the prison population, gang activity, and youth violence have also increased dramatically in homes where only one parent is present.

Discipline has historically been the father's responsibility. However, many fathers today don't discipline their children but leave the responsibility up to the mother, which communicates something extremely negative to the son. It says, "At least Mom cares enough about me to correct me, so I love her more." Some fathers never discipline their son because they have not yet invested the proper time necessary to gain the son's respect. You cannot make a demand on the child until you've first made an investment in him. Young boys are concrete thinkers; they think about places, people, and things. This makes it extremely difficult for them to have faith in anything, even discipline. Thus, their faith has to be seen through the example of a man they are around for them to truly grasp the concept. One of the greatest things a father can do for his son is to show love and respect to his mother. Young men lose respect for their father if they don't see him giving their mother the love, consideration, and respect she deserves. However, it can also contribute to young men disrespecting their mother because they view their mother as weak for not standing up to their father. They emulate their father by attempting to challenge their mother in the same way they previously saw their father challenge her. Naturally, boys think of their father as the one person they need to perform for, emulate, and impress. When these fathers are not present, the way the boys view themselves is distorted.

The absence of fathers can negatively impact the actions of young men in countless ways. They sometimes do things without truly understanding why, which causes them not to trust themselves. Actions of this nature limit their ability to form intimate relationships because they project the mistrust they have for themselves onto others. The first step for them to trust themselves is to believe that their needs, feelings, and emotions will be responded to with respect. They need to know they can be vulnerable and trust others with their secrets. This sense develops at the core of the relationship with their fathers.

Just as women are encouraged to be comfortable and intimate in relationships at the cost of their ability to express anger or behave assertively, young men are encouraged to be powerful and independent at the expense of their skills at intimacy. A man's fear of failure and discomfort with intimacy comes from his need to have others affirm his competence. A young man's greatest fear is failure, and his greatest need is respect. Many young men sell drugs to fulfill this need in their lives. They use this activity as a way to gain respect, status, validation, and prestige. All of these are voids to replace what they never received from their father.

Children from fatherless homes account for:

- 63 percent of youth who commit suicide.
- 93 percent of all homeless and runaway children.
- 85 percent of children who exhibit behavioral disorders.
- 71 percent of all high-school dropouts.
- 75 percent of all adolescents in chemical abuse centers.
- 70 percent of juveniles in state-operated institutions.
- 85 percent of all youth sitting in prison.[19]

The epidemic of fatherless homes has increased at an alarming rate. In 1920, 90 percent of all American children had their fathers at home; in 1960, 80 percent had their fathers at home; in 1994, only 34 percent had their fathers at home; and in 2003, only 16 percent had their fathers at home.[18] The percentage is steadily decreasing, and whatever the reason for this tragedy, we can clearly see that it has a devastating impact on our children. Several assumptions can be made regarding why fathers choose to abstain from their children's lives or why they aren't welcomed. However, it's proven that in most impoverished areas, fathers are discouraged from family involvement by social welfare laws that reduce or eliminate support if fathers are in the home. This forces families to eject the male presence to get a check.

Analyzing how the government enforces financial child support might lead us to believe that the male income is considered more important than the male presence. I'm not suggesting that men shouldn't be financially responsible, but encouraged visitations in conjunction with financial support would be much more effective for the overall success of our children. It's disturbing that society views fathers based on their economic resources rather than their overall character toward their children. Men who conform to this way of thinking underestimate their value and worth in the lives of their children. Many are deceived into thinking that as long as they are providing financially, they meet the requirements of being a good parent, while other men feel they have nothing of true value to offer because they can't provide anything financial.

Neither view considers that children possess more confidence when they know they can physically and emotionally depend on their fathers. In both cases, when financial support is the primary concern, the child suffers because the father is focused on himself rather than the child. Some men today feel their role as a man has diminished altogether and they're no longer needed; if a baby is wanted, sperm banks can be substituted. The security men once provided can be replaced by home and car alarms, along with self-defense classes. The entertainment that men provided to their children is now lost to video games, and the financial support that once helped to define his role is overshadowed by government assistance or the mother's salary.

There comes a time when men don't care about what strangers, coworkers, friends, in-laws, or anybody else thinks about them. When their children recognize their flaws, it's the ultimate wound to their ego. Men know they sometimes work too much, are too prideful, have too short a fuse, or simply fall short on the Dad Meter. Deep down inside, they know that being a good father is the most important job they could ever have. If they don't do it right, they know there is a significant flaw in their masculine armor. It's understood that real men don't just produce children, but father them as well.

The children who are stuck between warring parents feel trapped and confused to a degree. They see no way out and many times feel their life will always be filled with hardship. They see or hear about the struggle of one parent being magnified by the other in a demeaning way. Parents who speak in anger to their children or around their children never realize that all children recognize that "mommy plus daddy equals me." When they hear something negative about one of their parents, they feel they're hearing about a part of themselves who they'll one day become or are already. This causes mixed emotions to flare up, and in most cases, young people don't know how to deal with them.

Those children who aren't taking out their feelings on others violently have discovered a new way. They've turned to the Internet. Here, people are forming closer relationships with strangers across the globe than with family members in the next room; online are people who will support, encourage, and justify retaliation on those responsible for the confused emotions these young people might be experiencing. In addition, young people can go online and find love, support, comfort, encouragement, and reassurance that doesn't exist because they have no idea that the person they're chatting with may be a sex offender who's looking for his next victim.

Access to the Internet has been a double-edged sword that has cut, healed, helped, and destroyed the lives of millions. It's more powerful than ever, because the world has become so dependent on the Internet that life is unimaginable without it. Youth today can't even picture what life was like before the Internet came along. They understand that it's also a coping mechanism to deal with life's problems that the adults in their lives have been neglecting to help them with. It's common today to see young people on the Internet for hours, not spending even ten minutes with their parents. You even see young people out with their parents, still not spending quality time with them because they're constantly sending text messages or surfing the Internet from their cell phones.

As parents, it's our duty to find out why children are turning to technology instead of turning to us. What is it they want that we're not giving them that they think technology is providing? In most cases, it's sincerity. They want someone who cares what they think, who gives them time that's not rushed, who shows genuine concern about what they're interested in, who listens without interruption. They want someone they think understands them. "They don't try and understand me" is one of the most common phrases I hear teens use all across the country to describe why they don't talk to their parents and why there's conflict between the two. Young adults are looking for someone to relate to them and let them express what it's like to be them in a way they know will always be accepted.

Young people hate rejection, and so do adults. However, young people experience it with much greater frequency than adults can imagine. When they want to talk, they're told "Not right now"; when they want to share what excites them, they're brushed off with, "Can I look at it later"; when they ask for their parents' time, they hear, "I'm busy"; when they ask how they look, they're told, "Fine, now can you let me get back to what I was doing?"

When they ask, through their actions, "Am I a man?" they're forced to look at television to find the definition, and it doesn't exist there either. When they ask for help, they're told, "You can figure it out on your own; I did and look at me," which isn't always encouraging from the young person's perspective. When they ask, "Do you love me?" they hear, "You know I do, even though I hardly ever tell you or show you." When they ask, "Do you notice what I do?" they hear "I don't care, as long as it doesn't cost me money or inconvenience me in any way." Even when children ask for more water or maybe more food, they hear, "You can't still be thirsty; haven't you had enough to eat?" These rejections are what they feel and experience on a daily basis, which most adults are unaware of.

The Internet has become a much safer place for them to go and share because they will never hear someone tell them "later," "not right now," or "you're bothering me." This is why so many young people pour out their heart and soul to someone they don't know and couldn't recognize in a lineup of serial rapists, on places like MySpace, Facebook, and Xanga.com, to name a few. They will bare all to total strangers and share intimate details about their lives that their own parents don't know. Why? Because some of the people on the Internet have taken the time, expressed genuine concern, and are getting to know our children on a personal level. Unfortunately, some of the people on the other side of their computer screen are studying our children for the wrong reasons. They are learning their habits, their likes and dislikes, their favorite music, restaurants, and places to go, all to gain their trust and one day destroy or even end their lives.

It's time we wake up and be what our children need us to be and stop pushing them to the Internet to get the attention, reinforcement, and love we should be providing them. MySpace, which is by far the most popular social networking website in the world, has over 106 million subscribers between the ages of fourteen and thirty-four, and gains five million new subscribers each month.[52] Young people can create a MySpace account in less than a minute. There is no real way of verifying the information provided, so in most cases youth indicate they are older, and some adults often indicate they are younger. If you're on MySpace and are younger than fourteen, you have the option to make your profile visible for everyone to see or private so only your MySpace friends can see your profile, which won't show up in search engines. This makes it much harder for parents and adults to view what's going on with their children online, if they aren't linked in as one of their MySpace friends. It also makes it much easier for predators to pose as youth and hide their profiles, to make themselves less likely to be caught while soliciting youth, who might be younger than their profile age suggests. This age group is particularly vulnerable since they are more likely to be naïve about potential predators with whom they're sharing personal information.

There are countless incidences of youth having been raped, sexually assaulted, and even murdered by someone they met over the Internet. These youth make themselves easy targets, because far too often they put all their contact information on their MySpace pages, from the name of their school to their phone numbers to their city and state or even their home addresses. When teens meet, many of them don't ask for each other's phone number or email addresses anymore, they ask for each other's MySpace profiles, which in most cases provide significant personal information. What youth fail to realize is that these accounts can never be completely deleted. Even after subscribers delete their personal profile page, screen captures can trace back to their page forever. However, to these teens, the benefits of socializing outweigh the potential harm.

MySpace users often deceive themselves that their experience is going to be like the Las Vegas philosophy, what happens in Vegas stays in Vegas. However, MySpace is much different because what happens on MySpace doesn't always stay on MySpace. To these users, the reward of social popularity outweighs the risks imposed on them. The process of finding new friends, often complete strangers, for the sake of having the most friends, is called "friending." And for most teens, it's the glue that makes them stick to MySpace. On their profile pages they express their interests, thoughts for the day, likes and dislikes, as well as their values—all through language content, music, photos, and videos of themselves and others, for the world to see. They create links to one another's pages by naming each other friends, while feeling obligated to post a public comment on these pages because they were asked to be a friend. These comments are the ultimate tool to get dates, random sexual partners, bad information, as well as false validation from one another.

People use MySpace to become more popular to the world and will do whatever it takes to make that happen. On most MySpace pages the average teen places sexy poses with provocative looks, and comments on their page that will easily send the wrong message to a pedophile, who might be connected as one of their "friends." Some youth even go as far as posing nude to increase the visitors to their profile page, which ultimately increases the number of MySpace friends they receive, all in the name of popularity.

Every day, we put on clothes that convey something about our current, past, or future mindset, which defines our identity: what we do as a profession, what social class we'd like to be perceived to fit in, as well as our interests. Young teens usually begin to actively engage in this type of identity production as they turn from parents to peers as their primary influence. Youth who begin to participate in the broader social world become obsessed with fitting the way they want others to perceive them. They learn this by trying out different performances on their videos, photos, and page content. They use the comments others post as feedback to modify their dress, the way they pose, and the language they use to better transmit the intended persona.

This new form of peer pressure through technology is like nothing else that has ever existed. Addiction is what many young people feel when it comes to staying connected to socialization with their peers. Schools face many challenges due to the MySpace phenomenon: the safety of students due to predators, the cyber bullies who attend their schools, online rumors spread about students and teachers, and certain incidents that have happened around the world that were fueled by MySpace, which schools don't want to happen on their campus. Schools that haven't banned the use of MySpace during school hours have students who check their accounts between classes, during lunch and study hall, and oftentimes before and after school. The social networking site has become a vital part of their everyday lives, even those who don't have a computer in their homes.

Parents who have computers in their homes and allow their children to use them should always monitor this activity. Computers should be in a central location where there is an open space, not in the children's rooms, in offices where they can close the door, or in rooms that others rarely access. Parents should set time limits, while clearly communicating the expectations of what's acceptable and what's not. All parents should also be aware of how to check the history on the computer, which provides information on every website someone has gone to on that particular computer. I highly recommend that everyone who has a computer in their home install protective software. This helps to eliminate much of the unwanted danger that comes with random Web pages that pop up on computer screens, which really pique young people's interest.

It's good when parents know where their children are, but it's more important to know what they're doing. They might be in the next room and lost in cyberspace without their parents having a clue, and it could actually be worse than if they were physically lost. Being physically lost at least lets parents know that something is wrong, while being lost in cyberspace can not only be hidden, but can put an entire family's safety at risk because of their address and other pertinent information being placed before the world.

Social networking sites like MySpace aren't all bad. They have the potential to provide positive information that can impact people's lives in major ways. For instance, teachers on MySpace can post notes, comments on each day's lesson, and activities related to their subject matter that could further assist their students in learning. Using MySpace in this capacity could give students the chance to revisit information for an upcoming test and process the content so they could better understand it. To further connect with youth, libraries can create MySpace accounts as a way to interact with youth in their communities. They could include links from their page with quick and easy access to the library's catalog and other helpful research tools. Teens who normally wouldn't use resources from the library could now go through MySpace because they're already familiar and comfortable with technology and would see this resource as a part of the social network they're currently connected to.

Librarians who control the MySpace account connected to youth in their communities could host MySpace workshops for parents, teachers, and other members in their community about the benefits and dangers of social networking in teens' lives. Forming a teen advisory group would help make this education process a success. The youth who make up these groups could be heavily involved in conducting these workshops to give the true perspective, instead of the limited perspective that adults often provide. After all, the young adults are skilled in the social networking arena and would teach adults about the pros and cons, possibly more effectively than the adults could teach one another. This would also be a great way for parents, teachers, and students to all come together and develop plans on how these social networking skills could be implemented to positively foster the relationships needed for the students' success.

Law enforcement officials and technology experts can also be a part of these workshops and can speak from their points of views on how to help teens stay safe while participating in social networking online. A good way to hold the youth accountable and educate the adults at the same time is by using the MySpace pages of the youth on these advisory boards as examples to demonstrate the positive ways young people can use social networking tools. These libraries could also add value to their website and MySpace pages by having links to online safety and library resources. As a part of the workshop offered to adults as well as youth, a significant amount of time should be spent on showing teens how to decide whether or not to accept those who want to be their MySpace friends or reject them.

If something of this magnitude were held over the course of one day or several days, the impact would be tremendous. Each session could be video recorded and serve as a model for what communities around the world could implement in their area. Young people who serve on these advisory boards could show adults how to upload the videos to the library's website as well as the MySpace pages. In doing so, young people would be playing an integral role in being the solutions to their own problems with the assistance of caring adults.

KEY POINTS FROM THIS CHAPTER

CHAPTER 5

ESCAPING THE VIRTUAL TRAP

WHY WOUNDED BOYS THINK THEY'RE HEROIC MEN

CHAPTER 5

The media serves as a young man's best friend and his worst enemy all at the same time. It can assist him in denying his true self for the sake of acceptance and popularity among his peer group. In essence, the media helps him become something or someone he's not. Every day we see how it has successfully captured the minds of young men and stirred up their imaginations. The media's ability to influence its viewers can be extremely dangerous to our society. When we perceive what we see or hear in the media as absolute truth, without question, our youth become susceptible to inappropriate or false information. This in turn develops their attitudes as well as influences their behavior, therefore determining their outcomes, and all based on opinion and not fact. The immaturity of young people makes it easy to capture their attention, to build on their imagination and inaccurate belief systems. They experience self-imposed pressure because they're trying to emulate the latest media imagery of masculinity as a means of validation.

Many young boys become so dependent on media imagery that they develop unrealistic expectations. They expect media to empower, heighten, and intensify life, which is often an unattainable goal. These assumptions are derived from their search for manhood and masculinity. In video games and on the Internet, true manhood is exemplified by great physical strength, aggression and bravery, and desirability by all women. Young men focus their attention on this imagery to create the great "elsewhere" that can only exist in their minds. Because this place in their mind is intangible, it keeps them searching for something more. Imagination becomes the rubber band without resistance, because it's never ending. The further they go in their thought process, the more the imagination extends its boundaries to compensate for what the mind has created.

Unfortunately, young men use their imaginations and fantasies as a means to escape mental pressures. Doing so triggers excitement and anticipation, which often creates addictions. These young men begin to physically respond to fantasized sexual encounters, as well as the anticipation of looking at pornography. The power of fantasizing is the primary window that opens males up to addictions, and when it no longer provides the needed escape, they add other risky behaviors to enhance the experience.

In his last interview with religious leader James Dobson, seventeen hours before he was to be executed, convicted serial killer Ted Bundy unveiled the agony of his addiction to pornography. He explained how it started when he was a child. As a young boy of twelve or thirteen, he discovered pornographic magazines in a dump near his home. He was instantly captivated. In time, he went from viewing soft porn to becoming more addicted to violent porn in magazines and videos, which eventually led to an obsession with seeing women being tortured and murdered. Within the addiction, he developed a craving for something more that provided a greater sense of excitement. This thirst for excitement became more potent, more explicit, and more graphic. He then reached a crossroad where pornography didn't go far enough to satisfy his fantasies. Just beyond the line of reading or looking at pornography is committing an act itself, which allows an individual to step over the line from fantasy to reality.

In this exclusive interview, Bundy did say that he didn't blame pornography for all the murders he committed; he took responsibility for everything he did. However, he stated that the real issue was how this material contributed to molding his violent behavior. He agreed to do this interview to warn society of the dangers of hard-core pornography and to tell how it was one of the steps that led him to murder innocent women and girls. He said that, while incarcerated, he'd met several violent men who were deeply consumed by their pornographic addiction. FBI studies on serial homicides over the past thirty years continue to conclude that the most common interest among serial killers is pornography. Bundy believed that many young men just like himself were loose in towns and communities around the country, whose dangerous impulses were being fueled daily by violence in the media, especially sexual violence.

The reality is, just as with Ted Bundy, pornography and the portrayal of sexuality in the media can fuel any young man's thinking to affect his actions. In this day and time, pornography can reach into anyone's home and grab hold of them, youth as well as adults. Although most people rightly condemn Ted Bundy's behavior, those same people walk past magazine racks full of the same media that send youth down the road toward becoming a Ted Bundy themselves. Pornography can no longer be viewed as harmless fun that does not threaten our young men. If anyone has credibility regarding this issue, it would be Ted Bundy. The fact that obscene images can influence one's mindset to the point of acting as he did should be enough to raise red flags.

I've spoken to several young men in detention centers across America who are addicted to pornography and aren't initially aware that they have an addiction. When I share my life story and get them to open up and talk, their comments are exactly the same: they now know they have an addiction to pornography but started off thinking that what they felt was just a normal process of manhood. Many of these young boys have one thing in common:

they're developing a secret hatred toward females. Why? Because these young men want to be in control at all times. A young man understands that his attraction to certain images of women gives them a power that he greatly despises. His sexual urge for women constantly controls his thoughts, actions, and desires. In his mind, he knows that women are much more disciplined in the area of sex than he is, and he wishes he had that same control. He desires women and wishes that he could control their desire for him in return.

Many young men are deeply confused about sex because they are exposed to harmful movies and pictures of nude women and don't understand what's taking place in their minds as a result of this exposure. Many are programmed to think, based on movies and images, that the male is supposed to be dominant over the female, but from the young men's own experiences, they know that's not exactly the case.

I once spoke to a group of sixth-grade students at Yorktown middle school in Columbus, Ohio, about puberty and the different things that take place in their bodies during this time. Among this group was a young man who appeared to be very uncomfortable when we mentioned that we would cover issues involving girls. He even became disrespectful to the female presenter who was assisting me. The program involved spending five days with this group of young people, so I got to understand this young man more as time went on. He was known around the school for bullying and terrorizing little girls. I didn't really recognize this until the third day I was there. I noticed that all the girls that he picked on were pretty, light skinned, and had long hair. Immediately I thought, he's picking on them because he has a crush on them, but the way he treated them pointed to something more. When certain girls would come around, it seemed as if he was instantly consumed by violent thoughts.

After witnessing this strange behavior, I asked his teacher if I could take him in the hallway to talk about what I observed. After strategically getting him in the hallway without creating a distraction, I asked why he was so mean toward certain girls. The first thing he said was, "Because they think they're the boss and they can get people to do whatever they want because of their looks." This comment was a red flag for me because it was clear his behavior had nothing to do with what these girls were doing, but everything to do with how they looked.

Earlier, one young lady had gone to sharpen her pencil by his desk, and as soon as she came near him, without her saying a word, he began telling her she was stupid. I brought this to his attention while we were out in the hallway. His only comment was, "She is stupid." When I asked if he disliked other girls he said, "No, just them." I probed further to understand who he meant by "them," and it turned out he was referring to girls who had the same personality traits and physical attributes as the one in his class. I asked why he didn't like them, and his response validated my thoughts. He said, "I don't like how they make me feel. When they come around, my body parts start feeling weird, and it makes me feel uncomfortable, so I act mean." At this point, I knew he had been exposed to something other than these girls that caused him to feel this way.

What he was experiencing was a trigger, something that activates certain emotions when a specific stimulus is present. I asked him if he ever saw girls like this outside of school, and he said, "I saw them a few times on these movies that my uncle let me watch." It was safe to assume based on further comments that the movies he was referring to were pornographic. The stimulus was light-skinned females with long hair, which triggered certain emotions to surface. This boy's uncle's questionable attempt to educate him about sex had influenced his negative behavior toward a specific group of females. After discovering what was going on with this young boy, I immediately shared stories with him about my life and what happened to people I knew who were exposed to these types of movies and pictures in magazines. I was very careful, because I could tell he had high regard for his uncle, and I didn't want to come across as disrespectful. After speaking to this young man in the hallway, I explained the situation to the teacher and advised that his parents be notified and that he get some form of counseling. Without the proper treatment and attention, his issues with girls would only get worse as he began to deal with older women.

Unfortunately, pornography is one of the primary sources of education that young males receive regarding sex, thus becoming the central mechanism establishing their sexuality. It's critical for young men to learn about sex from well-informed caring adults. Regardless of what society and the media might say, parents are still the number one influence in children's lives regarding sex. There is no way to totally eliminate all exposure to sex, because we live in an oversexualized society. However, when high expectations are placed on these young men and they are equipped with the correct information, they're better prepared to make informed decisions to stay protected from these negative influences.[9] It's very important that responsible adults stay mindful of these potential downfalls because they're not just limited to young men.

Every day we hear about pastors, preachers, CEOs, coaches, and men in even more prominent positions getting caught up in pornographic addictions. These men didn't plan on one day becoming addicted to pornography, but what they once thought was under control gradually grew into an addiction over time. Seductive pictures that technically meet the description of soft porn saturate our society every day, especially on the Internet.

These images are even present in advertisements that cater to women. My wife at one point received Victoria's Secret catalogs, which seem harmless to women, especially those who aren't aware of how the male species is stimulated. However, based on my conversations with young boys and men across the country, revealing pictures, even innocently intended, are something that many secretly struggle with. The male species is stimulated by what they see and can become easily aroused by images of this nature, especially boys who are curious about sex and men who have not set proper boundaries in their lives. When the catalogs first began to arrive at my home, I would either put them under a stack of papers or I would throw them away. I had to take the advice that I often share with others, which is, it's a lot easier to stay out of trouble than to get out of trouble. Eventually, I asked my wife to cancel the catalog and view it online instead, and she did because she understands the visual stimulation process of males.

I've spoken with several men who became addicted to pornography after months of viewing magazines of women posing while wearing their bra and panties. They went from glancing at the magazine, to studying the pictures, to anticipating it in the mail, to wanting to see these same women with nothing on. This eventually led to them seeking more. In essence, what these images are doing is renting space in the minds of young men, which frequently are overtaken by flashbacks. The images go from renting space in the mind to owning space in the mind, which eventually sends a notice of eviction to the morals and values this person has. Unfortunately, the male can vividly recall sexual images hours, days, months, and even years after viewing them. If adult men who are happily married understand the possible negative effects of catalogs or magazines that come in the mail for their wives, imagine what young boys who constantly experience sexual exposure of this magnitude must be dealing with. They're allowed to go on MySpace and watch music videos that are practically three to five minute pornographic promotions.

Females in these videos have no inhibitions, and their actions closely resemble those in pornographic movies. The only difference is that they keep a very small portion of their clothes on, while moving provocatively, trying to entice anyone on the other side of the camera, even young, immature boys. Why are young men allowed to have access to material like this, oftentimes at home? Some might see this kind of exposure as harmless, but most people are aware of the elevated testosterone levels in young men. However, the harmful effects of addiction are the farthest thought in many adults' minds, even when they consider the effects of hormones. The problem comes when young boys start to develop an appetite for seeing more scenes with women showing their bodies, either on the Internet, in videos or magazines, or maybe directly in their neighborhoods and communities.

The sexually focused media that's become omnipresent subjects youth of all backgrounds to a premature loss of their innocence. Unfortunately, what's on the Internet and in the lyrics of music is winning the battle over the minds of our young people. The constant exposure in video games, music, and the Internet shapes their identity, especially when they don't have responsible adults present to teach them anything different. These images have a profound influence on their desires, attitudes, choices, and outlook.

Most people aren't aware that media contains hidden words, pictures, and sounds, referred to as subliminal messages, that influence consumer behavior. The most common form of subliminal messages glorify sex and power, which directly speaks to the issues of abuse of women. Those who are entangled in this web of pornography addiction most often are blinded by deception, thinking that what they're into is harmless, that what they crave is normal. This is equivalent to someone who tells a lie for the first time and feels it was a big deal. However, the more lies he tells, the more natural it becomes until it's a part of his normal lifestyle and is no longer a big deal.

The best thing adults can do to minimize this exposure to pornography for young boys is to become more aware that it exists. Parents and even teachers who understand the way males are stimulated can now direct males toward positive visual stimulation, thus replacing the enticing sexual images with positive images that reflect the power and purpose of our young men. An example of this could be to show them movies or powerful pictures of men in history who reflect positive behavior, morals, and values.

Above all else, one thing holds true: our young people are always searching for someone to follow, even if it's in the media. They're constantly deceived by certain media regarding what manhood represents, and they believe it to be truth because many have no men at home modeling healthy behavior in order to combat the lie. One member of my board of advisors put it best regarding media influence. When speaking to a group of students, he asked, "How would you know who my son was if he walked through the door?" The students gave various answers, including "He would look like you," "He'll dress like you," "He'd act like you," "He'll talk like you," etc. He then put it back on the students and said, "Just as you can tell me who my son is, I can tell you who your daddys are because you look like them, you act like them, you dress like them, you talk like them—and when you see them on TV, you run to them, just as my son runs to me." Unfortunately, this describes who has the greatest influence on the lives of many young people today. The daddys that many of these young people are emulating are digital. These digital daddies lead and guide America's youth, as well as youth around the world, every day. Adults must be able to see it is crucial not to be replaced by characters on TV or leaders who have more influence from the grave than many adults have in person.

Tupac Shakur, a famous rapper in the early 1990s, died in 1996 by gunshot. Young people who weren't even born when he was alive still listen to his music and dress like he did, even today. Why? Because he gave them a sense of identity as well as something to be a part of. He started a movement called Thug Life, and young men from all over the country began to follow it. Before he died, he spoke of how this movement was going to exist long after he was gone. Tupac was often quoted saying that he was a voice and not an echo and that his voice would be the spark that ignited a change in the world. He spoke into the lives of young people and identified with them on their level. He brilliantly used the past pain in his life to relate to their current situations. Instead of learning from his past experiences, however, he used them to justify rebellion toward authority. The problem came when young people did whatever he said, simply because he spoke with more force and passion than most of their parents and teachers did. It's no secret that the lyrics in Tupac's music sent negative messages, but the fact that he was passionate and shared his pain was and is the persuasive factor that this young generation follows. This is where adults come into play, because we have to be just as passionate and persuasive when expressing our love to today's youth as those who passionately glorify lifestyles of pain.

Young people follow others who are completely sold out about what they believe and live a life that reflects it. It doesn't necessarily have to be someone who's presenting good information, which is evident in what we see in youth today. As long as people are passionate and convincing, young people are likely to follow them, especially when there are no parents at home providing positive messages to combat the negative messages seeping into their lives. A good rule to follow is that every hour spent on the Internet or listening to much of today's music should be followed up with at least fifteen minutes of something positive. That could include things like reading, listening to positive music, or talking about something positive with you, their caregiver. When youth develop this habit, it helps create a balance in their lives and helps them remember what reality is. As parents and caregivers of this nation's youth, we all have a tough job ahead of us when fighting against negative influences. However, always remember, the battle is not lost unless you accept defeat.

KEY POINTS FROM THIS CHAPTER

CHAPTER 6
TAKING BOYS CAPTIVE

HOW PUNISHMENT CAUSES PAIN FOR SOME AND PROFIT FOR OTHERS

CHAPTER 6

Recently, society has seen a glimpse of the seed that has been planted in the hearts of young boys. Unfortunately, this seed is watered and cultivated by today's new-generation gangs. The origin of violence in young men begins when they believe their needs are not being met and desperately seek out solutions, as a tree with dry roots seeks water of any quality. Many youth falsely believe they can prevent others from teasing or making fun of them by inflicting physical harm. Fear, anger, and frustration lead to violent behaviors. The lack of adult focus or concern on these issues only waters the soil in which violent behaviors grow. Sadly, once these behaviors are engrained by years of reinforcement, there are few resources available to help, and a common answer is incarceration, as evidenced by the growing number of young men imprisoned each year.

Rather than sentencing our young men to a life behind bars, however, we should look for alternatives, such as counseling and community outreach and volunteer programs. Take a close look in your area at how much more money is being spent on prisons than education, as well as the number of corrections officers hired compared to the number of teachers eliminated each year. The estimated cost to house a young person in prison for one year in the United States is more than $40,000, compared to $9,866 to educate him or her. As schools close, more prisons open, and there are more opportunities for criminal activity among youth, the question that should be asked is, how did we get here? When did we see the need to spend more on incarceration than education? Why would anyone think the best option is to throw youth away and lock them up just to become someone else's problem? It all comes down to a few things, with fear being at the center of them all. The reason more money is spent on prisons than education is based on fear.

If we're honest with ourselves, those fears include the fear of being harmed by those we don't understand, the fear of not knowing how to deal with others who are different from us, the fear of getting out of our comfort zones to actually witness the lives of the less fortunate, and the fear of being challenged in ways we might not be equipped to handle. These fears make it easy for us to invest more in prisons than education because prisons remove the problem from our presence and shift responsibility to others. As a society, we have created a problem that we're now afraid of but aren't sure how to deal with. This problem is and has been how to control the uncooperative young male. The real solution was never really pursued because prison offered an easy way out. If more money were spent on education than incarceration and more knowledge was given to educators on how to transform these young men with potential, fear would be replaced with understanding.

Often, when an immature boy feels as if no one understands him, he acts in destructive ways, if for no other reason than to gain attention. To him, any attention is better than none, even if it is for bad behavior. Unfortunately, when he engages in bad behavior, it tends to be counterproductive, and adults never take his intentions into consideration, only his actions. His destructive actions only perpetuate and justify others' preconceived beliefs about him and his future. In many cases, the pattern of destructive and violent behavior leads to incarceration, which provides the first chance many young men have ever had to try to find out who they are and where they went wrong in their life. The problem, however, is that most prison facilities offer nothing more than a negative environment and further opportunities to get into trouble, including with drugs or gangs. As a result, many young men spend the rest of their lives in prison. Very little, if any, effective rehabilitation is available to young men in prison.

For years, prisons across the globe have been inundated with juveniles who have committed crimes and criminals who have committed crimes as juveniles, both of which are treated, viewed, and valued the same. The difference between the two is this: criminals have repeatedly committed crimes of destruction or violence against others, while juvenile offenders may have simply skipped school for the second time or committed some other minor offense.

Prison systems create jobs for one part of the economy at the expense of freedom and opportunity for another. Communities profit a great deal from having prisons in their area. The rural and predominately white areas where prisons are located have the opportunity to increase their share of federal grants and political representation. The prisoners housed in their prisons are added to their census figures for financial benefits. Meanwhile, the urban communities the inmates leave behind lose funds as well as political representation.

African American males make up only 6 percent of the country's population, but for the first time in the history of this country are greater than 50 percent of the penal populations.[19] If our society could be honest for a moment, we might conclude that young men, not just black young men, might be more valuable to us in prison than in society. This theory is based on the increase in laws to put them in jail as well as several financial factors. Take a look at how much money is spent keeping them in prisons. As mentioned earlier, over $40,000 a year per inmate is spent to incarcerate young men who are labeled criminals. Less than 15 percent of this amount is spent on programs to correct the underlying behavior that led to their incarceration.

While incarcerated, these men are encouraged to work, making anything from license plates to furniture. They are given paltry wages as low as workers in developing countries, while the products they produce are sold for premium dollar. The prisons use their labor as a means to bring in enormous profits. Many of the men are untrained, which decreases their ability to succeed once they are released, setting them up for a likely return.

The prison industry is a $40-billion-a-year business, and many companies have begun to tap into their share of these funds. Many prisons are private, run by corporations whose sole purpose is to make profits. The Wachenhut Corporation, today known as G4S, has been among the top in this industry for several years. The U.S. government hired them to manage and run jails and detention centers across the country. At one point, they became the nation's second largest for-profit prison operator with contracts abroad. George Wachenhut and the three partners who started the company were all former FBI agents.[37] These connections could lead one to suspect a conflict of interest between the prison industry and lawmakers. Prisons are big business, especially when the government guarantees payment for each inmate. Life sentences become much more attractive, as do longer sentences and shorter parole, for this very reason. The stockholders of companies like G4S are only interested in their investment. To some degree, they welcome longer sentences, prison expansion, and the idea of creating policy to fill these prisons, which are their investments. Due to the financial benefit of a full prison, cells at private prisons are filling up. There is not necessarily a correlation between criminal activity and the number of inmates in a prison.

Generally, private prisons haven't been interested in inmate rehabilitation because their main focuses are making profit, cutting costs by building larger prisons with less staff and reduced programs and services, and maximizing labor from inmates.

If prisoners were paid fair wages, they would have the needed funds once they were released to help them rebuild their lives. Their wages could also be available to assist with child care expenses for the prisoner's family, helping to reduce the burden on single mothers or any other caregiver left with the responsibility of caring for the prisoner's children with no additional support.

I frequently spoke to the inmates at a detention center just outside of Columbus, Ohio. After six sessions of learning about sex, marriage, character, self-control, their identity, and how to truly represent manhood, a foundation of trust was established. On occasion, I saw the former inmates in the community after their release. Several of them stopped to thank me and expressed their appreciation for my interest and instruction. As time passed, my invitations to speak at the detention center decreased.

My last opportunity was during the spring, which they often refer to as "peak season," since juvenile crimes usually increase around this time. When I talked with the activities coordinator of the facility, she told me in a discouraged tone that the number of young men they normally housed was down. My reply was, "This is good, isn't it?" She said, "Yes and no" and began to explain that when the numbers were low, the staff's hours were cut back because there was no one to serve. She also remarked that their facility lost funds when the numbers were down because they received money for each inmate housed there. When she picked up on my disgust at her comments, she quickly said, "It's great for the young men because they aren't locked up anymore."

As the months passed, I stopped hearing entirely from this particular detention facility. To me, this was a strong indication that their interest was in money rather than rehabilitation. The activities coordinator's words—"the numbers are down"—continue to ring like someone blowing a whistle directly in my eardrum. Unfortunately, the focus on profit and numbers rather than the overall well-being of young men isn't limited to Ohio, but exists in other parts of the country where for-profit facilities are located. People's livelihood is predicated on young men entering into the juvenile justice system.

Seventy percent of inmates are in for minor offenses that could be rectified in a more productive manner.[33] One young man I had the opportunity of speaking with explained why he was locked up. He said he had been caught skipping school for the second time and was sentenced to thirty days. Locking a child up for skipping school a second time is an unlikely solution to the problem. Some might believe that this would teach the boy a lesson and make him think twice the next time. In reality, though, he will go back to society more bitter, resentful, angry, and rebellious toward the school, school officials, and everyone he felt was responsible for punishing him.

When punishing or chastising young men, if the corrective measure doesn't correlate with the offense, they see no relevance. Every corrective measure that is taken should provide sense and meaning. If it doesn't, nothing is going to prevent the young person from repeating the same action. In most cases, the juvenile justice system doesn't provide the sense and meaning these young men need to deter their negative behavior. If it did, the repeat offender rate wouldn't be as high as 80 percent, or even higher in certain parts of the country. The majority of the young men in detention centers across the country will tell you they've been locked up more than two or three times.

Whenever I speak at detention centers, I always ask how many people have been locked up more than once, and most of them raise their hand. When I ask how many have been locked up more than five times, a few hands remain. At this point I let them know I don't even want to know anything above that number. The ones who don't raise their hands because it's their first time usually all say they think that after they're released, they'll be back. I joke around and ask them if they keep coming back because the food is good or if the people there are just that nice. Obviously I'm only kidding, but from their responses, they honestly don't know. If a young man who has been locked up as many as six times in the same system says he doesn't know why he keeps coming back, he is asking questions through his actions because he doesn't know how to verbalize them. The system he's directing his anger toward is not answering his questions but keeps locking him up, never solving the problem as he keeps repeating the same actions.

We must deal with the individual and not just the issue to identify the reasoning behind the continuous negative behavior. Jail may provide young men with more attention, discipline, and stability than their home life does. I heard about a young man who, on the day he was to be released from his third stint in jail, asked if he could stay. He was told that he had served his time and there were no further grounds to detain him. He then looked the guard in the eye and said, "I'll be back later on this week." He wasn't out for two hours before he was arrested for stealing from a local K-mart, near the home where he was released. It was later discovered that he lived with his aunt, who was on drugs and had different men in and out of their house since she utilized her body as a means to support her addiction. If this young man had been approached as an individual and not just an issue, his situation would have been recognized long before his fourth arrest, and something could have been done to intervene.

It's understood that once you're locked up you can no longer do what you want to do; you have to do what you're told or suffer the repercussions. This type of discipline is what young men desire, regardless of what they have to do to get it, even if it means going all the way to prison. It's their very nature to resist discipline, but it's the obligation and opportunity of their loved ones and caregivers to give them something to resist against. When they don't receive love, support, discipline, and encouragement at home, they go out into the world to receive it. The problem with the juvenile justice system is that it offers no real solution to positively change the mindset and situation of young men once they are released. The approach these systems take focuses only on the young men's negative actions instead of the positive actions they are capable of. When we look at them as how they are, they only get worse, but when we look at them as how they could be, we help them become what they are capable of becoming.

It's astounding to see how little money is spent on crime prevention programs compared to how much is spent on police, courts, and jails that respond to youth and juvenile crimes alone. There are always more punishment funds than prevention funds allocated for youth issues. Each year the United States spends $7 billion on building new jails and prisons.[25] Early intervention programs can prevent as many as 250 crimes per $1 million spent, while the same amount spent in prisons would prevent only sixty crimes a year.[48] This number falls much further if you take into consideration that youth already incarcerated are limited in further criminal involvement.

It's rare to see these young men tested or treated once they're locked up for any type of illness that could be contributing to their behavior, and in many cases, that is exactly what has led to their incarceration. It may be a disability they've had since birth that went undetected or a mental illness they developed over the years from repeated abuse.

In either situation, if policymakers had more interest in perceiving certain criminal acts as an illness, it would be treated more like an epidemic. When dealing with epidemics, we must discover a cure or risk infection ourselves. However, if the focus remains on keeping detention facilities full because each young man is a valuable commodity, this only perpetuates the vicious cycle of systematic slavery. As a society, we will always go in the wrong direction when we send our children to "correctional" facilities that offer little or no correction.

After they are released from incarceration, many young men are programmed to find violent, angry, rebellious boys as friends, rather than make those same boys enemies. In prison, they find some sort of comfort and common ground with the other prisoners, so surrounding themselves after their release with violent individuals creates feelings of familiarity, protection, and security. Gangs are a great example of this phenomenon. There are several gangs in different prisons in Florida, California, and Texas, and even in Puerto Rico and in various other parts of the world.

Members of prison gangs have just as much influence on what's happening on the streets as members who aren't incarcerated. They even recruit future gang members and issue direct orders from prison, with the sole purpose of ensuring the continued strength of the gang. Whenever any species feels insecure or threatened, they increase their numbers at a higher rate to ensure their survival. This theory has been the driving force of gangs since their inception.

For many young boys who come from dysfunctional families or have none at all, gangs are an alternative to a nurturing family, but in order to be a member, boys must swear lifelong allegiance and take a death oath. "They have very strict laws and guidelines that result in violations if the rules are broken."[3] If a member of a gang robs or kills someone without cause or permission from the gang leaders, it results in a violation. "Violations are also known as inner disciplinary punishment issued by the leaders of the group for violating the gang set's rules. These punishments range from performing menial tasks to physical assault for a set time period to death. Members of the different gang sets are required to follow all orders given by their leaders and failure to do so results in violation."[3]

Gang members are even given nicknames by the leaders as a means of representing their set. These new street names are in most or all cases ways that gang members identify themselves and others. They often don't even know each other's real name; the nickname holds greater significance. If they were to get caught by police, the exclusive use of these nicknames makes it harder for them to break one of the gang's laws, snitching. Gang members understand that telling on another gang member could cost them their lives. Nicknames also give gang members a certain psychological perspective about themselves. It's an identification of their physical description, stands in place of a signature, and often gives a clue to identifying their graffiti type.

Graffiti is a distinct way for gangs to communicate territorial limits, signal warnings, or publicize challenges to rival gangs. A challenge is issued when one gang puts its graffiti symbol on another gang's territory. The crossing out of another gang's symbol could lead to serious retaliation. Seeing graffiti in public places is an indicator of gang activity in the area. The analysis of graffiti is an excellent tool in understanding behaviors, attitudes, and social processes of certain segments in society. Most violent gangs are comprised of black, Latino, and Hispanic males. Black males ages twelve to twenty-four are almost fourteen times as likely to be homicide victims as members of the general population.[40] In various parts of the country, the figure for Hispanic and Latino males is only slightly lower. The power that gangs have over young men to make them knowingly risk their lives is amazing.

Even though evidence proves that the peer group has the most influence on young people because it's where they spend the most time, it's still puzzling that gangs can hold such power over them. What becomes more interesting is the number of whites in recent years who have formed gangs or joined existing ones. For years, society has viewed young black and Latino male groups as aggressive gangs, whereas young white males congregating together have been considered assertive groups. Violence in these gangs is on the rise because they're seeking the identity and respect that long-established gangs have built over the years. They long to be feared and known by their accomplishments; they desire to be set apart by their actions, not their cultural and racial differences.

However, Latino and Hispanic gangs above all others have reached the status of "enemy number one" throughout the United States. The large influx of Salvadorian refugees to Los Angeles in the 1980s because of the twelve-year war in El Salvador directly and rapidly increased gang activity between Latino and Hispanic youth. Existing gangs in Los Angeles saw the Salvadorian youth as targets, which led the newcomers to desperate measures. They quickly formed cliques for the protection of Salvadorian refugees and immigrants. These cliques became known as Mara Salvatrucha. The word "Mara" is a Salvadorian term for gangs, and "salvatrucha" is the Salvadorian term for guy.

Prior to migrating to California, many of these refugees had ties to violent gangs in El Salvador, were members of paramilitary groups, or had been trained as guerilla war fighters. Their civil war had given them much experience in using explosives, firearms, and booby traps. Most of these refugees settled in the established

Hispanic neighborhoods of the Rampart area of Los Angeles. They were not readily welcomed or accepted and felt threatened by the local Hispanic gangs. Like the Crips, they originally united for protection but quickly developed a fierce reputation for being dangerous themselves.

The complexity of this gang is that while they are flexible, they also have very strict rules and structures for members, and they are identified by several names: Mara Salvatrucha 13, MS-13, MSXIII, Sure~no, Sure~no 13, and even Sur 13. The number thirteen symbolizes their alliance with Southern California Hispanic gangs. They view the number thirteen as lucky because M is the thirteenth letter in the alphabet and is synonymous with La eMe, or the Mexican mafia, predominately a prison gang that controls most Hispanic street gangs in Southern California.

MS-13 gang members sometimes wear blue and white, representing the flag of El Salvador. They also wear tattoos all over their body, including their face, with names and symbols representing their identity. When authorities began recognizing MS-13 members by their appearance, they disguised themselves in several ways: putting bandanas in their back pockets rather than their heads, and using the numbers 67 or 76, because their digits add up to 13.[11] However, not all members are overt; some are less visible and therefore more dangerous.

Because of their increased violent crimes, threats, and attacks against law enforcement officials, MS-13 is considered the most dangerous gang in the United States. Their members' criminal activity consists of, but is not limited to, gun running, drug smuggling, immigrant smuggling, theft, drug sales, arson, hostile turf takeover, extortion, racketeering, and hits for hire. Their signature in some murders is to dismember and decapitate corpses and leave a note attached. They have committed some of the most gruesome crimes this country has ever witnessed, as a means of sending messages to other gangs and authority figures alike. MS-13 has even threatened certain governments for cracking down on gangs by killing youth and leaving notes attached, saying more will die if the authorities don't back off. These threats are taken very seriously and have struck fear in the hearts of many.

The gang's growth over the past few decades in California and Washington, DC has been alarming. Mara Salvatrucha has expanded to Michigan, Virginia, Texas, Florida, Maryland, Oregon, Nevada, Utah, Oklahoma, Illinois, New York, Alaska, Georgia, Arkansas, Rhode Island, and North Carolina. All of these states, as well as fifteen others, have been infiltrated by the strong pressures of MS-13 members. They also have an enormous amount of representation in El Salvador, as well as Guatemala, Honduras, several other South American countries, Mexico, and parts of Canada. Originally, only Salvadorians could become members of Mara Salvatrucha, but they now have members from Ecuador, Guatemala, Mexico, Honduras, and even Africa. These inclusions have made MS-13 more sophisticated in many respects because the diversity has made them much more difficult to identify.

It's estimated that there are more than 250,000 MS-13 members in Central America, with more than 36,000 in Honduras alone. This gang has global representation, with new membership joining by the thousands, especially in the United States. MS-13 has spread from Southern California to major cities and rural communities all over the country. This gang is so dangerous because of its mobility; when there is pressure on them in the United States, they just move and set up shop in different countries. If they're experiencing heat in El Salvador or Honduras, they move to Mexico. It's known that they control much of the Mexican border. In addition to smuggling drugs, they collect money from illegal immigrants to help them cross into America. U.S. and Mexican authorities estimate that this gang has over two hundred active cells (groups of at least twenty members) operating in states that border Mexico. Rumors have surfaced that high-profile terrorist organizations have made contact with MS-13 for assistance in crossing the borders. MS-13 is unique for being known by several names, maintaining active ties with members and groups in El Salvador, and verging on becoming the first gang in history to be categorized as an "organized crime" entity.[22]

Sadly, statistics overwhelmingly indicate that youth are disproportionately affected by social problems linked historically to crime. These social issues include the breakdown of the family, poverty, family stress, separation of family, unemployment, and poor education. In essence, this summarizes why these youth turn to gangs. About 95% of all hardcore gang members are high school dropouts.[3] Most, if not all, gang members come from communities that lack strong fathers or male figures. The attractiveness of gangs stems from the misguided urge of fatherless males to seek membership, acceptance, pride, recognition, and a sense of power wherever they can find it. Arrest rates for juvenile males are astoundingly higher in low-income communities for that very reason.

Youth also join gangs for love, respect, discipline, money, recognition, belonging, and a sense of identity. They sometimes feel rejected by society, so they create their own subsociety to have a place to fit in, oftentimes feeling invisible until they commit a crime. In most societies, boys have to prove their manhood, but girls simply develop into womanhood. Gangs instantaneously offer a false sense of manhood to their members. Gangs also allow young men who continuously commit wrong actions to be supported by others who share the same level of conscience. Together they give positive reinforcement to negative behaviors in an attempt to dignify their failures. Gang members often see competition as being more beneficial than cooperation as a way to gain control and power. What many of these young men never take into consideration is that when you have power it's evident, but when you lack power, you do everything within your power to make it seem as though you have it.

The harsh reality is that gangs offer a sense of community for rejected young men, financial gain for the poor, adventure for the idle, action for the restless, protection from outsiders, and the opportunity to connect with powerful older males. In no way am I advocating gangs, but just painting a realistic picture. Gangs offer young men what they aren't getting from home and other nurturing environments.

For instance, let's imagine a teenage boy living with his single-parent mother and perhaps younger siblings. This mom is working two jobs just to pay bills and can't afford child care or a complete meal every day. The older brother is left to care for his younger siblings and scrounge together meals for them. After perpetually doing without, and watching his mother struggle even though she works two jobs and never spends time at home, selling drugs becomes attractive to him; he sees that by doing so, he can make a lot of money very quickly and have those things he is doing without. This is one of the main reasons young men join gangs: the false hope that all their money problems will disappear.

"On an initial investment of $2,500 worth of cocaine, using two readily available household chemicals, $10,000 worth of 'crack' can be produced. In areas of high demand it's not unusual for a gang to 'turn over' (increase the profit on) its initial investment by a factor of four."[3]

In a sense, gangs fight over turf in the way corporations do, whether it's shelf space or geographical location. Both are seeking large profit margins, whether they're selling drugs or other products. Some gangs are now starting to become more high-tech by sending members to college. Some of these students actually do better than the general student population because they have others directly depending on them for information. Gangs that have risen to this level of sophistication are much more difficult for law enforcement or social workers to tap into. It is far more complex to win our young men back after they've already pledged their allegiance to such a family.

My second year in college I met a gang member, Lenard, who lived on campus. Over time, he and I became good friends. His life was intriguing, and every time we met up I always found myself asking him questions about gang life. He once explained to me what his tattoos meant and often said he regretted what he referred to as his lifelong ink scars. Eventually he began to trust me enough to share bits and pieces about how to join a gang. The two popular ways were to either be "jumped in" or "sexed in." Jumped in is a process in which several gang members jump on and beat up the person who's joining. They hit, kick, stomp, and do whatever else can cause physical and mental harm. Lenard also explained that being sexed in was strictly for females, and girls who chose this route weren't respected as much as girls who were jumped in. I must admit, at the time I began to think, "Wow, they have everything they need, from power, to women, to money and each other."

Very quickly, I found out how intriguing gang life could be from seeing only one aspect of it. However, the closer I became to Lenard, the more I realized that most gang members have no idea what they are getting into when they join, and once they understand more about life, they realize the downside but feel powerless to get out. One day, when I was probing for more information, he became agitated and said, "Chris, you have control over your life." He began to shout. "My life is not my own—it's what they say it is." It was shocking, interesting, and scary to see him act in this manner, which was well out of his character. After a moment of silence, I didn't know what to think, say, or do because I had never experienced an incident like this. At that moment, I knew Lenard felt what so many young men around the world feel: a sense of fear, pain, and emptiness that nothing else can fill except the protection, support, and love from a father. The only difference between Lenard and others who experience this feeling is that the way he chose to fill the void might cost him his life if he ever tried to escape it.

As he calmed down, he told me that he never knew his father; the only man in his life was his uncle, to whom his gang regularly sold drugs. As a child, he had always admired and looked up to his uncle. When he saw the only man in his life who fit the description of a strong male being controlled by something this gang offered, he wanted to be a part of this group that possessed so much power. He joined when he was fourteen, and by fifteen began selling drugs himself, to his uncle. "Our family was in constant turmoil over my uncle's habits that instantly got worst when I became a drug dealer. They all knew I had something to do with it, but the money felt better than the guilt I experienced from my uncle's downfall," he said. Lenard later told me that the most painful experience he ever had was watching three members from his gang beat up his uncle. They held his head against a curb and kicked him in the back of the head so that his gold teeth came out because he owed them money for crack.

Lenard's stories made me understand that this lifestyle was nothing I wanted to be a part of, but most young men who join gangs never see the reality before they join. I just so happened to come in contact with someone who trusted me enough to share the truth. One of the last times I saw Lenard, he said he had to leave school because certain things were going down. He wouldn't tell me what they were because he said it was in my best interest if I didn't know. I respected what he said and didn't ask any more questions. His dropping out of college really affected me because he was a much better student than I was but wasn't afforded the opportunity to finish. Crossing paths with Lenard led me to take my college experience more seriously. His story is also why I travel across the country speaking to young people so they'll never have to think about an escape route from a gang—because if I have anything to do with it, they'll never join to begin with.

Young people who join gangs often hear that the only options gang members have is to end up in prison or in a grave. Lenard never showed signs of being suicidal or even talked about suicide, but I can only imagine that sometimes he wished he could just end it all. Often, young men who do go to prison experience constant anticipation that their lives will end. They worry about encountering a rival gang member in prison or being turned on by their own members. Gang members rarely trust one another because their relationship is based strictly on a survival-of-the-fittest mentality. It's unspoken but understood that at any given time if there is a call on their life (orders for a hit), they'll be forced to defend themselves against the same members they once called family. This makes it impossible for them to totally trust, love, support, and interact with one another without constantly being on guard.

The gang of choice that many young people call their new family will have an unparalleled influence that will intensify how they view the world based on the culture they've now been adopted into, which is extremely negative. We as parents, teachers, counselors, and friends have the power to change this cycle, but only if we take responsibility and stop waiting on everyone else to correct the problems.

KEY POINTS FROM THIS CHAPTER

CHAPTER 7
THE WIZARD OF OZ

REVEALING THE SECRET BEHIND THE SCREEN

CHAPTER 7

Not every young person who has emotional problems is confronted with a gang lifestyle, but there are still dangers from seemingly innocent sources. Another form of media that arguably has an effect on the thoughts and actions of our youth is violent interactive video games. The virtual graphics are so advanced that they almost cause one to touch the television to make sure the characters stay inside the screen. The technological advancement in video games has blurred the line between make-believe and reality for many people, not just children. Every day it seems something new appears to entertain our youth—in other words, keep them company—while adults go about their daily business, blissfully ignoring their responsibilities.

I'm not insinuating that every parent who has purchased an iPod, video game, PlayStation or anything of this nature is irresponsible. However, it's indisputable that many children spend far more time learning about the newest game consoles than about morals and values to protect them from games that display tremendous violence. The frightening reality is that too many young people lack the basic skills needed to foster healthy relationships. This is because they spend more time interacting with video games, the Internet, or some other form of technology than with real people. They are missing the face-to-face interaction that requires a whole range of interpersonal skills necessary to nurture successful relationships.

Young men who are allowed to lose themselves in video games have a difficult time distinguishing when the game is over. It's easy for them to transfer their actions toward people in a video game to people in real life. The fact that some video games allow players to act out crimes and reward them for doing so should also be a source for major concern.

A frequently cited example is the extremely popular and controversial Grand Theft Auto Series by Rockstar Games, in which a principal game activity is carjacking, or stealing a car. Once a car is stolen, the player can run over pedestrians. The player may also purchase guns to shoot at and kill rival gang members (or pedestrians) as he completes missions for what are known as crime bosses. The game is also controversial for its attitudes toward and depiction of women: players can pick up a prostitute and have sex with her, then his "health" in the game goes up. As this act of sex is taking place, the rear bumper of the car bounces up and down to simulate the sexual act. If the player wants to get back the money he's spent on this prostitute, he can shoot and kill her, and the money is immediately returned. Further, the game also implies racial hate crimes among specific groups. It involves a gang war between Haitians and Cuban refugees, and the player often serves both gangs to plot against and kill one another.

As responsible adults we can look at this and think, this is too ridiculous for anyone to believe because everyone knows your health won't go up from having sex with prostitutes and there will always be consequences for killing someone. I totally agree, and many who play this game may never go out and shoot someone, join a gang, or have sex with a prostitute.

But what might young people be learning from constant exposure to these video games? They learn to do whatever comes to mind, you have a greater chance of escaping punishment than facing it. Young people who are obsessed with these types of games transfer the concept to other areas of their lives. Even though they may never kill someone, many young people push the limit to see what they can actually get away with. Their thinking is, "I can get away with this because at least I'm not shooting or killing someone." Anyone can justify doing something wrong, especially when he compares himself to others who are doing more extreme things. Repeated exposure to these games lessens the shock value of the actions, be it murder or sex or theft. Once the mind perceives these actions as "normal," taking the next step of performing the actions in reality is not far away.

The most effective way to reduce or diminish the likelihood of our young men imitating the behaviors in these video games is for them to see the reality of such behaviors being punished. They also need adults who will sit them down and use this modern-day media as a teaching tool about what not to do as well as what's best to do. The more exposure young men have to this type of media, the greater chance they have to develop a mindset of fear or anger.

Exposure to violent video games has an adverse affect on how young men view, treat, and relate to the opposite sex. Young boys who are allowed to immerse themselves in such video games unconsciously and consciously degrade women and view them as objects to satisfy their desires and allow themselves to be abused in the process. This way of thinking fosters the association of violence with pleasure. The young men become emotionally detached and are completely desensitized to the pain and suffering of others.

Some critics in the media have singled out various video games as major causes of many of the tragic school shootings committed by youth. In 1999, teenagers Eric Harris and Dylan Klebold killed fifteen people and wounded twenty-three others before taking their own lives at Columbine High School in Littleton, Colorado. Michael Carneal, a fourteen-year-old boy from West Paducah,

Kentucky, shot and killed three students and wounded five others. All three boys were said to be addicted to the violent video game Doom. In this game, players take on the role of a space marine, "one of Earth's toughest, hardened in combat and trained for action soldiers," as the game's literature says. According to the manual, the marine seems to have been forced into a security or unimportant staff position: "with no action for fifty million miles, your day consisted of suckin' dust and watchin' restricted flicks in the rec room." All of a sudden something evil takes place, and he's forced to fight various cyber demons and risk being consumed by monsters or forced to kill them as his only means of escape. After shooting and killing several demons in what the game refers to as hell, he's set to face the ultimate "Spiderdemon" that masterminded the invasion. If he can destroy this last demon, a hidden doorway back to Earth opens up for him, the hero who has "proven too tough for Hell to contain."

Continuous exposure to action-packed video games increases the need for more powerful images in order to receive the same heightened emotional response the game initially offers.[28] The next step in seeking this level of stimulus is by transferring the virtual reality to reality. A study by A. Crag et al. says, "The 14-year-old boy arguing that he has played violent video games for years and has not ever killed anybody is absolutely correct in rejecting the extreme 'necessary and sufficient' position, as is the 45-year-old two-pack-a-day cigarette smoker who notes that he still does not have lung cancer. But both are wrong in inferring that their exposure to their respective risk factors (violent media, cigarettes) has not causally increased the likelihood that they and people around them will one day suffer the consequences of that risky behavior".[53]

These types of games should be viewed as offering destructive advice that becomes relevant when real-life problems present themselves. Now, let's venture farther into the callousness and sadism of the creative psyche in the world of video games. The Columbine incident, which left the world in a state of shock, with parents fearing for the safety of their children and students fearing that they could be the next victims, has now itself become a video game. Super Columbine Massacre RPG was created by Daniel Ledonne, who grew up in Alamosa, Colorado, and was a student nearby at the time of the Columbine school shooting. Upon starting this game, participants are greeted with the following statement: "Welcome to Super Columbine Massacre Capitol RPG! You play as Eric Harris and Dylan Klebold on that fateful day in the Denver suburb of Littleton. How many people they kill is ultimately up to you."[46]. You're given the option to choose whether to use guns, hand-to-hand weapons, or explosives, all of which were used in real life. Once the game has started, it's impossible for you to escape. You're limited to two options: either kill the enemy or die. This game could be the most dangerous of them all because it gives a step-by-step account of how the event took place, detailing events from the time Eric was awakened by his mother and phoned Dylan, to meeting in Harris's basement to plot the school bombing that would take place prior to the shooting. [46]

This video game is a breeding ground for destruction. Young adolescent boys who fit the description of outcasts and loners now have the recipe to cook up Columbine disasters all over the world, and this game can be downloaded directly to your computer from the Internet. Many young boys who deem themselves misfits and who have been bullied turn to video games for comfort. The creator of the game, who identifies himself as a misfit, stated his game was an indictment of our society at large. This statement has since been lived out as a reality.

On September 13, 2006, a twenty-five-year-old young man identified as Kimver Gill went on a shooting rampage in Montréal, Canada, at Dawson College. He fired sixty shots, nine of which resulted in the death of eighteen-year-old Anastasia Rebecca de Sousa, a student at the college. The random rapid gunfire also ripped through the flesh of nineteen others, leaving six in critical condition. Gill then turned the gun on himself and took his own life. A short suicide note was obtained from his body. The shooter was found to have a profile at www.vampirefreaks.com, under the screen name "fatality 666," where he logged in for the last time at 10:35 a.m. the day of the shooting. There he professed his dislike for Republicans, God, churchgoers, religion, and homophobes. He also disclosed his love for violent media. Among his favorite video games was the highly controversial Super Columbine Massacre RPG. Police found his black Pontiac Sunfire parked close to the school where the shooting took place. In it they found a notepad with directions to other schools that he obviously was targeting.

The Dawson school shooting, as did the Columbine incident, ignited a wave of school shootings around the world. Three days after the shooting took place, Raliv Rajan, a former schoolmate and friend of the Dawson school shooter, sent emails to three of his acquaintances praising Gill's actions and hinting that he might do the same. He was arrested for making death threats and then subjected to a thirty-day psychological evaluation. Only two days after that incident, a fifteen-year-old boy was arrested for announcing similar intentions on the same website Dawson College shooter Kimver Gill utilized. He was planning an identical shooting at a high school west of Montréal. One might argue that these are isolated incidents, but facts demonstrate otherwise.

In the two months after the Dawson College shooting, there were twelve other school shooting incidents reported around the globe. Of these incidents, two people were wounded, one critically, twenty-seven were injured, and nine were killed. One incident in particular occurred two days after the Dawson College shooting, in Green Bay, Wisconsin. Three teenage boys were arrested on suspicion of a shooting attack at Green Bay East High School. After police confiscated several weapons from their homes, the young men confessed to being depressed and admitted to a fascination with the Columbine shooting.[4]

Males, ranging from ages thirteen to fifty-three, committed all of these violent shootings. Most of them shared similar backgrounds: they had been bullied, were viewed as outcasts, identified themselves as misfits, and were considered loners. Many young men in today's society fit into these categories, though not to the same degree, but in time they could reach these same levels. Violent events like school shootings fuel the minds of thousands of young men who don't know what to do with their anger, frustration, bitterness, rage, or depression. They give the youth ideas about how and where to channel their feelings so others feel the wrath of their pain—by hurting people. They want others to empathize with their hurt, even if it means victimizing them.

Most of the school shootings dating back to more than a decade ago were inspired by some form of media, whether it was video games, the Internet, movies, music, or the publicity about previous school shootings. The young shooters all identified with some form of influence outside themselves as a last resort to end their agony. Among the most popular is rap and rock music. Even when young people feel cast out by society, have nonexistent relationships with their families, alienate themselves for protection, and feel as though no one understands them, they still identify with some form of music. Many youth will tell you that music affects them, and when they want to be in a certain mindset, they play specific music to usher them there. Music may be the only universal tool with the power to influence our behavior.

One reason video games are so popular is that, in conjunction with the graphics, music is also played as background stimulus to heighten the experience. Some people will tell you they just listen to the beat, that the lyrics would never affect them. One fact remains true of all music: it enters people's conscious or subconscious minds without their permission. Those same youth who say they only listen to the beat can be heard quoting the lyrics verbatim. What's even more interesting is that the people who are responsible for putting out violent lyrics and video games will openly tell you that they don't allow their own children to consume these products. This would be like Henry Ford saying he would never let his children drive any Ford vehicles because they're too dangerous. If the manufacturer wouldn't trust his children with his own product, why should we trust ours with it? Video game and music producers don't just sell products, success, and fame. They sell the promise of a lifestyle, which is exactly what many young people today are blindly pursuing.

Interestingly enough, the U.S. military has cashed in on high-tech media to meet their own agenda. Video-game training is now producing the ideal candidates for the battlefield of the future, because the increasing advancement in technological involvement with weaponry further distances the operator from the target. For years, the military has used first-person murder simulator games to train their soldiers, the same ones many young children have access to. The same training that's being given to soldiers is being consumed by today's youth, who are too young to enter the military.

Military officials have become aware of this and, for quite some time, the military has been recruiting soldiers through video games. As a matter of fact, the Government Communications Headquarters (GCHQ), the surveillance arm of the intelligence services, was the first spy agency to embed advertisements for new recruits inside computer games. The advertisements appear as billboards in the fictional landscapes of games like Tom Clancy's Splinter Cell: Double Agent. The advertisements are not written into the games themselves but are fed into games when they are played on personal computers and Microsoft Xbox 360 consoles that are connected to the Internet.[54]

Industry figures suggest that the ads will reach a mostly male audience between the ages of eight and thirty-four. GCHQ hopes to "plant the idea in the heads of younger players" of pursuing a career in the secret services. "In 2002, The United States Army released a free-share online game called America's Army. Players that register, and who agree to certain conditions, are allowed to have their play performance reviewed by real-life recruiters looking for potential enlistees. The game, however, was mainly designed to convince possible recruits to join the U.S. Army, not test them. America's Army is the first computer and video game to make recruitment an explicit goal and the first well-known overt use of computer gaming for political aims.[55]

Let's look back at all the school shootings. Many of them were accurate shooters, though they had no experience except for the video games. If you analyze the ages of the GCHQ's target market, it could raise the question of whether video games are connected with school shootings. One may argue that video games didn't cause these shootings, but one thing is for certain: based on accuracy alone, the shooters definitely received practice from the games. Government Communications Headquarters could very well have great intentions for recruiting youth as future secret service agents, but is the potential risk worth the reward? A spokesperson for GCHQ described the potential recruits it wanted to reach as "computer-savvy, technologically able, and quick thinking."

This strategy proves more effective than the conventional means of attracting people, and the move to video games demonstrates the increasing sophistication of the intelligence agencies' approach. Kate Clemens, head of digital strategy at GTMP worldwide, GCHQ's advertising agency, said, "Online gaming allows GCHQ to target a captive audience.... Gamers are loyal and receptive to innovative forms of advertising."[56] This is also more cost effective and reaches a far broader audience than traditional methods. However, what Clemens failed to mention is that most online gamers are unaware that they're a captive audience to those preying on them for military purposes.

Video games, which were at one point considered harmless entertainment for children, have come a long way since the introduction to Pacman. Does the fact that GCHQ places virtual advertisements in these games disturb you at all? It should. Others may argue that video games are creating a generation of young people with highly tuned motor skills, and there is research to suggest that gun-firing video games can improve players' hand-eye coordination. However, this could be an unintended side effect. The real aim might be to create individuals to control a robot army. At the very least, the games are an effective method of desensitizing young people to war, killing, and bloodshed. The overwhelming evidence is that the negative effects of violent video games far outweigh any positive benefits.

In May 2007, British newspaper *The Guardian* reported that Google may use games to psychoanalyze Internet users. According to the article, "The patent says: 'User dialogue (from role playing games, simulation games, etc.) may be used to characterize the user (literate, profane, blunt or polite, quiet, etc.). Also, user play may be used to characterize the user (cautious, risk-taker, aggressive, non-confrontational, stealthy, honest, cooperative, uncooperative, etc.)'".[57] This type of access removes all privacy barriers that people used to rely on. Therefore, what would stop military recruiters from building up psychological profiles on all young online gamers? Before any initial interview, a recruiter would know how individual recruits respond under pressure and how best to influence them to get the desired result. Scenarios could be targeted to induce specific psychological conditions. With the addition of email, browsing history, and data-mining software to monitor searches, the recruiter would have all the information and tools necessary to manipulate and assess potential soldiers.

The initial free release of America's Army, the official game of the U.S. Army, used the services of GameSpy, also known as GameSpy Industries, a division of IGN Entertainment, which operates a network of game websites and provides online video game-related services and software. It is currently controlled by News Corporation, a company chaired by mass-media mogul Rupert Murdoch. His media empire includes the FOX television networks in America, British SKY broadcasting, and *The Sun* and *Times* newspapers. Consequently, he has an undeniable influence on the way information is presented through these channels to the general public.

Murdoch also happens to be a member of the Council of Foreign Relations (CFR). Formally established in 1921, the CFR is one of the most powerful private organizations with influence on U.S. foreign policy. It has about four thousand members, including former national security officers, professors, former CIA members, elected politicians, and media figures. It essentially dictates foreign policy and promotes its hidden agenda to the public by maximizing the number of media companies it controls or influences through mergers, acquisitions, and control of editorial staff.[58] It's clear that Rupert Murdoch, as well as the elite groups he heads, has a vested interest in promoting the war agenda and is very influential in seeing that news stories are presented in a way that wins support from the public for his agenda. It's also clear that his corporation goes to great lengths to accomplish their agenda, even by using the latest technology to assist in military recruitment.

As often as possible, responsible adults should minimize children's exposure to the negative impact of violent computer games and media. It's vital to be aware of just how interconnected technology companies, media corporations, and politicians actually are. We need to also be aware that these organizations do not have our best interests at heart. In short, much media exposure among youth occurs without the parental supervision necessary to protect them from what they're being exposed to. This is the primary reason why young people are so defensive; they feel they have to protect themselves against all the unknowns by themselves. Young people need assurance that they can enjoy life as children and not have to deal with adult situations as youth. They desire the comfort of adults who will passionately stand up for what's in their best interest, especially when it involves protecting them from harm of any kind.

KEY POINTS FROM THIS CHAPTER

CHAPTER 8

THE BREEDING GROUND OF SUCCESS

WHAT PARENTS ARE DOING TO GET THE RESULTS THEY WANT

CHAPTER 8

Too often, young men's positive accomplishments are overshadowed by the negative actions of other young men. Sadly, many boys act out because they know it will result in attention: media attention, time in a courtroom, or time in a principal's office. Their negative actions serve specific purposes, including gaining respect from their peers for challenging adults or the law. Sadly, the majority of these young men don't have any positive influences in their life, so they'll take any attention, even if it's for the wrong reason.

But what about the boys who do the right thing? Why is it that they are pushed behind the curtain? Oftentimes, they're overlooked, and their accomplishments are rarely noted. This goes back to the theory that the squeaky wheel gets the grease. Studious, respectful, and courteous young men are put on hold until adults are finished dealing with their problem peers. Worse still, others tease them because of their positive behavior. Many of them are disliked because adults ask other children things like, "Why can't you be more like him," which creates enemies for the straight-steering boys. Most of the time, adults aren't even aware of this. These boys frequently experience pressure to do wrong just to fit in and not make others look worse by having their behavior compared to someone who is making better choices.

I'd like to take the opportunity to shine light on a few young men who've made the right choices, and to include a bit of advice from their parents, who helped them forge their path. Whether you have a trusting relationship with your child or students or you're at a point where you don't know what to do, the following examples may help you determine your next step. Following are interviews conducted over the past few years with parents who offer sound advice from their own experience.

Daryl and Star Hudson, parents of Daryl Hudson Jr.: Once you have children, all challenges become equal. None is greater than the other because all are significantly important. You have to be consistent with your children, and you must hold them to high standards. We've always wanted our children to be better than we were. It's tough raising children, especially young boys in today's society, to have good morals and values because of all the negative peer pressure. The one thing that we instilled in our son at an early age is the power that we have as parents versus the power of his peers. We are firm believers that fear and respect are the same thing. Based on the fear that he has for us as his parents, he would much rather deal with his friends than us as his parents when he got home from doing something that he knows he shouldn't have done. Not that children are going to be perfect, because they aren't. But when you're stern and consistent, they understand that by deviating from the plan there will be consequences to face.

For us, we taught our child that we all follow a certain plan, which consists of understanding that we all represent one another when we leave our home. We drilled in him that when we're not around he's a representation of us as a family. So to go outside of our home and act inappropriately displays that we as parents haven't taught him the proper way to conduct himself and that we allow this type of behavior. We have always believed that once he left our home, it didn't mean that he left us. He would still have us with him when he leaves the home, based on the values we expect him to share with others as our son. In essence, we taught him that deviating from the plan is acting any way other than what's expected from him when he's home.

The way to instill these values in your sons is by number one, being consistent and letting them know that you have standards that you expect them to meet. Just as in life, if you don't live by certain standards there will be consequences, the same applies in our home. Even if we don't want to issue a consequence, we have to based on the contract we've all signed in our home, which is if you veer off from the agreed-upon path, we have to push you back on by any means necessary. Because he understood this agreement, we didn't have to enforce many things on the contract because he knew it was in his best interest to follow the agreement. Parents might take this as a figure of speech, but we really write contracts out in our home. We had a contract for our son when he played basketball for Belleville High School regarding his grades. Before the season started, we agreed that if he got any Ds on his report card he was off the team, because we never even consider Es. After the first card marking he received two Ds, and we took him off the team, based on the contract that he signed. It really hurt us to make this decision, but we knew we had to deal with a man before we dealt with a basketball player. And speaking from a father's perspective, I literally cried, but I made him go and watch the games to allow him to see what he did to the team as well as himself.

It's very important to hold young men to high standards to keep them away from certain systems put in place to punish them. Not that these systems are wrong, but for us we'd much rather punish our son than to see him punished by others. To not hold our son to high standards and watch him fail would cause us to feel as if we've failed as parents, as citizens of the United States, and as a community. Standards are important to us to help assure that he becomes all that he's supposed to become, which is a law-abiding citizen who can contribute to his community, as well as his family. As a father, my goal was always to be the black male role model to my son that I never had from my father.

Something that makes us proud as parents is that our son never lost focus when others thought he couldn't play varsity basketball, Division 1 college basketball, or professional basketball—all of which he accomplished by holding on to the belief and support of the few that did believe in him and ignoring the belief of the masses who thought that he couldn't. He's currently playing basketball overseas on a professional level, but more important than that, he earned his physical therapy degree from Howard University, which is one of the best schools in the country, in our opinion.

A statement that he made that really stands out for us as parents, was when we asked him how is it that he's getting As and Bs in college but was getting Bs and Cs in high school? He said, "Honestly, I was lazy and didn't see what the both of you were trying to tell me at the time, but I see it now." This statement for us exceeded all other accomplishments because it allowed us the comfort of knowing that he really understood our intentions. It's easy to go out and get in trouble and waste your life, but it's difficult to discipline yourself for four years and get a degree. This is the primary reason why most young men never do it, but they need to.

In our opinion, the only way society is really going to change is by encouraging more young men to go to school and get their education. It might be a little harder to do, but it's the most rewarding. One last thing that we recently heard about our son from one of the teachers at his high school was about a time the male teacher was having problems with another student. The student swore at him, and he got up to go after the student, and our son stopped him and told him "Mr._____, it's not worth it." This teacher just shared this with us after five years and told us that he really believes had it not been for Daryl, he would have lost his job. That comment reinforced that we were and are doing our job as parents.

To help young men reach their full potential you have to be parents first and not friends. In our home, we always let our children know, I love being your friend, but I'm your parent first. We'll do what's best for you, not what you feel is right or what's best. We're going to protect you and provide you with what you need to be successful, because we've been there before. At times when you're a parent, your children aren't going to like you all the time, but that's when you know you're doing your job. As parents, we keep each other on task, because you can lose focus at times, but we had to be accountable. We do understand that all children don't have both parents and some are being raised by one parent, mainly women. It's key for both parents to be in their child's life, which many aren't because they feel they've done wrong and can't contribute or tell their children anything. These people feel like hypocrites, never realizing that a hypocrite is someone who did something wrong and is now allowing their children to do it—that's a hypocrite. When you know you've done wrong and you don't correct your child from doing what you did, that's a hypocrite.

The advice that we would offer to parents raising young men is to always stay consistent and set boundaries. Young men need these boundaries to maintain the parental fear that's missing in many young people today. At one point it was common to see a young man 6'6" fear his 4'7" mother when she instructed him to do something. Today you might see someone curse at his mother, disrespect his mother, all because of the lack of boundaries and consistency.

Starla Vasser, mother of Danario Barnes: The toughest challenges as a parent are trying to have open and honest communication with my son. I put the emphasis on understanding him more than anything because there are times when parents and teenagers just don't understand each other; they don't click. At times he didn't understand me and I didn't understand him, which is an aspect of parenting that some parents just go through.

It's also difficult when both parents aren't in the home. Even though his dad was in his life, it was still challenging because he wasn't in the home. So there were times when I had to be both mom and dad, and it made me feel as though a certain bond was missing, based on dual roles I felt I had to play at times. Mothers typically provide the nurturing and caring, whereas fathers tend to provide the discipline and modeling in a young man's life. I was trying to play the role of father so much that I may have been too hard and missed out on the nurturing and caring from the mother's standpoint, which essentially caused the emotional support to take a backseat.

I always tried to instill keeping God first in your life because without him, we would be nothing. Education was and is important, which has always been a high priority. Education wasn't a high priority from my parents' perspective, even though I knew the importance of it. So this began a driving force to impart this in my son by allowing him to understand that it was important to me. I tried to instill this by being the example, teaching Danario from my success as well as things I didn't succeed in. It's important to hold young males to high standards so they can become the standard for others who need to see real men. It's also important so they don't just settle and give less than what they're capable of.

Some of the things that he has accomplished as a result of the high standards are overcoming the barriers in life that he was faced with. Growing up in Highland Park, Michigan, is a struggle within itself, and to defy all the odds that were against him took a lot. He's always been an all-honor student from the time he started receiving grades and has taken great pride in it. This has afforded him a full ride academic scholarship to Kentucky State University, where he's just started his freshmen year.

As far back as I can remember, Danario has been a positive role model for his peers, especially those who came from the same neighborhood he was raised in. The high standards placed on him were preparation not only for college, but also life itself. It has put him in the habit of holding himself to high standards in all that he does, because this has been what was and is expected of him.

Parents can help their sons reach their full potential by staying involved in their lives and staying involved in their schooling. It's not good to just sit on the side and watch; you must be actively involved. It's also important to know their friends and be involved with that aspect of their lives as well. At times I'm sure I was extreme in this area, but my intentions were always good. When he turned fifteen, I felt like he needed a little more than I could give him at the time because I was a female. I felt like he really needed a male in his life to teach and show him what it was to be and grow into a young man. So I allowed him to live with his father for about four months, but it didn't go as planned, and he was back home. That incident reaffirmed the importance of a child having both parents in the home, and even if it's not possible, both parents should put their differences aside for the sake of what's best for the child. The relationship between his dad and I wasn't the greatest at the time, but because I felt that something was missing, I did what I felt was best at the time for our son.

The focus should always be directed on what's best for the child when considering any situation that could possibly affect him. It's no longer about the parent or parents, but the child who is in between both and sees that as a struggle in itself. Even the parent who isn't in the home should also play an active role in the child's life so he feels supported by both parents. Even if one parent isn't the best model or has a lifestyle that might not be pleasing to the other parent, it's still important for them to be involved. In most cases, the child doesn't see what the other adult sees; they just see "this is my mom and this is my dad."

Women, and single parents in general, who are raising young men by themselves, I would advise that they celebrate the other parent being in their lives. If they want to be in the child's life, do everything you can to help establish that relationship. I would also recommend that the parents keep an active role in what their children are doing, even if they think you're being the biggest pest in the world. Try and understand what they're doing in school and out of school, just so you won't be in the dark and you'll have an idea of what they're interested in and what's going on in their lives. They might not understand it, but at some point they will grow to appreciate you looking out for what's in their best interest.

I've always felt it was important for me as a parent to know who my son was with and where he was going. Not in an overbearing way, but more so out of concern. When he went away to college, I had to learn how to separate him from being that little boy that I had control over to this now young man who I had to trust to make decisions on his own. This was a challenge for me because I couldn't decipher the little boy from the young man. I still felt like he was to listen to me and do everything that I said. On the other side, he's feeling like "why are you trying to treat me like a child," and this is where I think both parents come into play. Although I was a nurturing parent, it was difficult for me to show it in the traditional sense that mothers do, because of the absence of his father in the home.

Ron and Kathy Tijerina, parents of Blake and Brandon Tijerina: (www.Theridgeproject.com) One of Ron's biggest challenges was being a father during his incarceration and making sure he behaved like a father and not just a friend. When a man is incarcerated, he doesn't want to push his children away, so he has a tendency to be a friend more than a parent. The three-hour family visitations made it difficult to maintain that balance because he didn't want to spend that time lecturing and disciplining his sons, Blake and Brandon. With the help of his wife, Kathy, he was often reminded that he must be a parent first and a friend second. In the back of his mind, he always worried his sons would resent him for always lecturing them and telling them what they should be doing at home.

Ron's faithful and supportive wife helped him maintain a balance of expecting their sons to do what was right and creating excitement to see their dad. The challenge that Kathy faced as a parent was trying to instill values and character in her sons, to make sure they truly embraced the values and didn't just behave a certain way to keep their parents from looking bad. A quote that she shared to reinforce her point said, "The best of leaders it will be said after all is said and done, we have done it ourselves." This quote has been the basis of the value system she and her husband instilled in their sons. They hope that when all is said and done their sons don't give credit to their mom and dad, but to God. It's only that relationship outside of themselves that matters most from their perspective. The thought process behind this belief is that long after mom and dad are out of the picture, these things still remain.

The values that Ron and Kathy wanted to teach their sons model the example that others need to see. Therefore, when people say they want to know what a man of his word looks like, they can point to their sons; they won't have to ask them what it means, they won't have to hear them talk about it, they can just watch the way they live. They've always wanted their sons to be young men of their word. The values they instilled in them have ensured that their sons won't lie to their parents; they might not tell them everything, but they won't lie. This allows Ron and Kathy to put great value on their sons' word.

With Ron in prison and away from home, another value that was important for them was their faith. They felt it was extremely important for their sons to know that they still had a father who was active, loving, and present in their lives—for them, this was God. These parents wanted their children to know that they didn't have to be perfect and that they would always be loved. They wanted the boys to know that God loves them unconditionally regardless of their actions and he is always there for them.

They instilled the values of being a man of his word and a man of honor by being that example in their children's lives. They felt it was far more important to model this belief than lecture it, while taking opportunities to discuss it as well. This teaching was 10 percent conversation and 90 percent "walk this way." Both parents felt it was important to have open communication with their sons and allow them to ask any questions that came to mind, even questions related to Ron's prison experience. Being real and being open was a key factor in their relationships with their sons. According to Ron and Kathy, "If we don't open up and share, why should they?"

Standards are important, because the higher the standard, the closer young people get to achievement. If you lower the standard or compromise the standard of excellence, it's human nature to think, "I'll shoot for this, but it's okay if I don't get it." If the standard is mediocrity and that's all someone is striving for, he's probably going to hit closer to the failure range than mediocrity.

However, if we raise the standard of excellence, they may not reach "excellent" but they may reach "great." The point is, the higher we hold our standards, the higher young people raise their sights. If they reach the mark, that's great, but even if they fall short, they can still hold their heads up. If all a child sees is a parent falling short—whether that parent is a drug addict or alcoholic or is experiencing mental bondage—that's the standard for their children. However, according to Ron, if this person is awakened or born again, the standard is the standard set by Jesus Christ.

Their sons, Blake and Brandon, often tell their parents about certain things their friends are struggling with, and on many occasions, they give their friends the advice shared by Ron and Kathy. In essence, this confirms that these parents' words didn't fall on deaf ears. According to Kathy, their sons have taken the foundation she and Ron gave them and built on it and are now helping others.

They have also taught their sons that practice doesn't make perfect, it makes permanent. Things that you do every day are things that will become a permanent part of who you are and of your character. We also relate this to family by teaching them that there are no perfect families, children, mothers, or fathers, but what we are in each other's lives is permanent. Our goal is to practice and work at working through things, being an intact family and people of integrity.

Ron shared a story about an apprentice and a monk. The monk says to the apprentice, let's go down to the city and preach. So they leave the monastery and go down to the city and walk for hours. When night comes, they go back to the monastery, and the young apprentice says to the monk, "I thought you said we were going to preach." The monk said, "We did, but we only speak if we have to."

This is a philosophy that they teach their sons about leadership: a true leader is one who can influence others without having to speak. This is how you hold a young man to high standards, by demonstrating those standards in action and showing what the rewards are. Young people are bombarded by images in magazines, on TV, and on the Internet that neither show the real consequences nor reveal the rewards of the lifestyle of a man of honor. They need to see more of what it means to be a man of your word, a man of integrity, or a man of honor. Many young men stray because they may have been taught good values, but they have not seen enough rewards and are then bombarded with negative influences.

As a result of this teaching, Kathy and Ron's older son, Blake, has committed to doing the opposite of what his generation expected of him: he's become a loving, responsible husband and father who works and goes to school full time, while balancing other activities. Blake is unique because he's become inspired instead of defeated by his own struggle. It's overwhelming at times for Ron and Kathy to see their son instill these same values in his children that were instilled in him. Their joy comes from knowing that their grandchildren will be the first generation of Tijerinas who will not join the welfare generation, the alcoholism generation, the drug addiction generation, or the domestic violence generation. Instead, they will be the first generation that doesn't need delivering from these things or need to experience them to know that they're unwise.

When their younger son, Brandon, was three or four years old, his dad went to prison, and Brandon told his mom he really missed sitting on his daddy's lap. He picked a chair in the house, and every time he sat in that chair, he pretended that his dad was sitting there and holding him. He would go and get a blanket and wrap it around him, as if it was his father's arms. He would sit there in contentment, experiencing the feeling that he felt when his dad held him during visitations. Kathy says that when she watches Brandon now, she sees that he wants the same warmth, that support, that security, and that love for everybody around him. He now travels as a speaker and is part of a band called Not Forgotten. Its message is centered around issues that youth experience, from suffering from eating disorders, to being fake just to fit in, to letting go of everything and trusting God, to learning to be the person God created you to be.

Brandon is also a humble giver, meaning he doesn't like getting attention for things that he feels he should be doing. According to his mother, Brandon saves up his money for an entire year to help out migrant youth and their families. No one knows he does this except his parents and the woman he gives the money to, who has access to these families. Brandon has shared that his reason for doing this is to help these people feel God's love and God's presence, as he has in his life. According to Kathy, his moments as a three-year-old boy in a chair, wrapped up in a blanket, allowed Brandon to feel God's love in his heart. This same presence is what Brandon now wants to share with others, because he knows that God gave him an experience that others need to feel as well. Brandon has an amazing heart of compassion and such a drive to make a difference in this world. Brandon is referred to as spider-man because he climbs the walls of life without letting those walls confine him—the walls of society, the walls of low expectations, the walls of being a young man in today's world.

Brandon and his brother have overcome several obstacles in their lives, including their father's imprisonment, a history of alcoholism and drug addiction on both sides of the family, and their mother's struggle to support them on welfare. As a result of what Brandon experienced in his family and among peers, he and a few friends started a group called The Abstinators. The name refers to abstaining from alcohol, sex, drugs, and other risky behaviors. Brandon courageously went around to schools, into the communities, and to parents to share his story and to explain that his generation has to expect more. He even went to a training session for guidance counselors to share his message.

Blake has founded a video production company called Scat Cat Production. His ultimate goal is to make documentaries on real-life hardship and the triumphs that come from overcoming them, even though the world may never know or see what families go through just to stay intact and produce honorable, healthy adults. He wants to highlight the people who have struggled and overcome the obstacles in their lives. Blake was also a featured speaker at a prison recently and spoke about rebellion. His message was that rebellion originates in low expectations; statistically speaking, he himself would be expected to follow in his father's footsteps and go to prison. He spoke about how he had to rebel against that expectation and remind himself every day not to fall into what was expected of him.

Ron and Kathy's advice to other parents is to always let their children know that they support them. Hold them to high standards, then make their goals attainable by guiding them through the process. They urge instilling in boys to always be men of integrity, and they connect that message to real-life situations. Even at the age of five, if they break something, parents should teach them that a man of integrity tells the truth no matter what. Other useful acts include taking out the garbage and making up their beds without being told. It's also important to allow young people the freedom to fail without making them feel they have plummeted and can never redeem themselves. If they feel this way, then they'll never try, for fear of failing. The standard should remain high, with the expectation that they will achieve it, realistically knowing that as they move forward, they may stumble and fall, that they're going to make mistakes. They should then own up to those mistakes, stand back up, and keep going forward.

Najah Brown, mother of Bacari Brown: As a parent, at different times I'm faced with different challenges. For an example, I can get overwhelmed with all the things I have to do, such as teaching, being a parent, and finding a balance. In most cases, my focus is on my son's schoolwork being done and making sure he's on top of everything. As a result, I might not put as much effort into my personal work, seeing that both require energy and effort. In most cases, I'm always opting to focus more on the parenting side rather than the teaching side in the daily accommodation of both.

Another challenge, especially when I'm tired or have a lot going on, is in the area of discipline. It gets frustrating at times because it's just me disciplining him. Running has become a great outlet for me in releasing frustration that I might have, along with setting a bedtime schedule for Bacari. Scheduling his bedtime at a specific time every night provides structure for him and it gives me something to look forward to daily, after he's asleep.

The times that I might feel frustrated, I openly communicate to him that I'm frustrated and that he's not helping any. I'll explain to him that I need him to work with me as a team and right now he's not doing his job and needs to step it up a bit. In most cases this works well because it gives him a chance to help me, help in the partnership, and gain positive reinforcement in the process. When I'm tired but still have to be what my son needs, music really helps with this aspect of parenting. We might sometimes put on music, from jazz to classical, that serves as a soothing background noise to calm us both down, and during this time he's usually playing with his toys quietly. And if he's not playing with toys quietly, I'll have him read, which he has gotten into and really enjoys doing. During these periods my goal is to have him engaged in something that has his mind working, letting him know that he can occupy himself with something other than TV.

For many parents, TV can be the best babysitter because children are quiet, they don't disturb you, and they're out of your way. However, turning on the TV is more like a habit. If you don't introduce the habit, it doesn't become something that the parent nor child relies on. Even though it requires more work, we might play board games to keep the mind stimulated and off of TV.

During the summers we usually get the cable cut off, which has allowed us to enjoy more outdoor activities, such as riding bikes, playing at the park, or even taking our dog for a walk.

What I value is being on top of things and being successful, which Bacari and I spend a lot of time talking about. We talk about him being a talented person and that it doesn't just come on its own and that it's a God-given gift. We also discuss taking responsibility for your own behavior. Whatever choices he makes are his choices, and it's not my fault or anyone else's for the choices he makes. This topic is always circulating among us because many children being raised by single parents are allowed to blame their behavior on the fact that the other parent isn't around. I even talk to him about never using his dad not being in his life as an excuse to misbehave, because again his actions are his actions. There can never be an excuse for anything he does, because the choice he makes is all on him as an individual.

Education and treating others with respect, especially women, is something that I highly value. I make sure he understands respect by judging his words and the way he treats others, because these are things that he will carry with him in his adult life.

I instill these values in him by talking to him often and using every teachable moment that we may witness. For instance, we may hear a conversation between a husband and wife or a dad and his child that might be negative. I'll teach him what's acceptable and what's not acceptable in these situations and explain why. As a result, these moments have given him the opportunity to express what type of dad and husband he wants to be one day. The conversation we have at home about what's expected of him and why is often reinforced by things we see in public, which makes the teachable moments that much more valuable and meaningful to him.

Things that he has accomplished as a result of me holding him to high standards are always being on the honor roll; he's never not been on the honor roll. He has been the first-place winner in three science fairs. He was also chosen to participate in a science leadership conference for a week at Northern Illinois University, called the young scholars program. He was nominated by his teachers for this position based on his grades and consistent leadership ability. In addition to playing soccer and baseball, he's also been a part of several plays that have been featured around Columbus, Ohio. He won first place in the Martin Luther King oratorical contest on the city, regional, and state level in Ohio. As a result, he'll be a featured speaker at the Dr. Martin Luther King breakfast in Columbus this year.

At the age of eleven, Bacari is determined, without the influence of others, to become one of the best lawyers the world has ever known. Barcari has presented poetry on the Tavis Smiley show and was invited by the Columbus urban league to attend a reception for Maya Angelou, where he was the only child in attendance.

The way that parents can help their sons reach their full potential is by holding them to high standards and encouraging them to do what they should, regardless of what others may say. I model this to my son because others feel I'm strict on him by minimizing how much TV he's exposed to. However, I know this is best for him in the long run.

As a teacher, I always observe the students who do really well, and generally they are the students who read often and are exposed to a multitude of things. My son and I have reading times, and we discuss what we've read. We also go to museums and travel when possible, because being well-rounded and having this exposure is key in a young person's development. A big thing that parents can also do is to get out of their comfort zone and expose their children to things that might not be considered popular within their culture. This positions children to be more comfortable and confident in any setting. It's also important for parents to show their children that they love them and to constantly reaffirm them.

It's also in the parents' best interest to encourage their sons to express their emotions and vocalize what they feel. When emotions are bottled up is when they start acting out in different ways and get aggressive, displaying the negativity that comes with not expressing themselves verbally. These are things that children don't usually do on their own; adults may have to prompt them.

The advice that I would offer to parents is to always be an advocate for your child at school, academically as well as socially. Understand the details of your child, like who their friends are and what activities they're involved in, and get to know the family of their friends and what the parents of his friends value. As far as education is concerned, it's critical for parents to be active in their child's schooling because it lets the teacher know that you're an advocate for your child and that you're an involved parent. The amount of involvement parents have in their child's life will also dictate the quality of education their child receives—not that they'll be given special treatment, but it will cause the teacher to spend a little more time and effort when dealing with your child because they know that you care about your child and value education.

Luke and Lonnie Edwards, parents of Luke Edwards: The toughest challenge that we have faced as parents has been our different parenting styles. Because we were raised differently, we have different viewpoints, and at times that causes us to agree to disagree and come to a mutual agreement that we feel is best for our son. From a father's perspective, discipline is one area where we specifically disagree at times, because Lonnie feels I'm too hard. I often revert back to how I was raised and do what I feel is appropriate to handle the situation at hand.

The most important values that we want to teach our son are to be honest, to fear the Lord, and to work hard. Nothing comes easy, and we've always wanted him to understand that whatever he wanted in life he could have. Any goal he sets for himself, he can achieve it, but hard work is necessary for this to happen. He also understands that he has to be honest at all times, because without honesty he can't get the proper help he may need. Leadership has also been something we value because we've always wanted him to be an independent thinker and not someone who succumbs to peer pressure.

The way that we instill these values is number one through communication. This is important, because many people grew up in homes where they feared talking to their parents. They felt like no matter what they said, their parents would not believe them or somehow think that whatever happened was their fault. So we always wanted to have the open communication with Luke that reassured him that he could talk to us about anything. This has built the confidence in us to know that we're going to provide him the correct roadmap to help him navigate through whatever situation he might face.

In addition to communication, showing him that we love him and have his best interest at heart has also been a way we instill values. Teaching him the importance of making your own decisions is also a key factor. We never let him get something just because somebody else has it because that starts the process of becoming a follower. We always have him give us a reason that justifies why he wants something, to make sure others are not influencing him. We try and use real-life situations to get this point across and communicate why it's important to make your own decisions and not follow those of others.

It's good for us to hold our son to a higher standard because the world is very competitive. If we hold him to high standards, when he gets in the world things will be much easier because he's used to being held to a high standard. If we raise the bar and expect him to work hard, his level of working hard will surpass the norm, therefore giving him a greater opportunity to reach any level of success he chooses.

Some of the things our son has accomplished as a result of being held to high standards include an award from the Van Buren public school district. He received this award for being student of the month for displaying outstanding leadership. He was also recognized by and received an award from the Wayne County Executive for outstanding student leadership. He was also nominated for the Young Scholars program and, as a result, went to Northern Illinois University for a week, where he studied CSI (crime scene investigation). Luke was the student body president for his elementary school and served as a peer mediator for the last two years, which consisted of listening and helping other children with some of the issues they were facing.

From an athletic standpoint, Luke was a regional MVP as well as a national MVP in baseball. These two awards were earned during his first season ever playing baseball and were obtained while playing AAA baseball, which is the highest level of competition for his age group. Recently he was invited by the Major League Baseball world series of youth baseball to play in Austria this summer and compete with youth from all over the world. His first year playing Pop Warner football, he was invited to the all-star game, where he competed against others who were selected to the all-star game in his age group. He attended a five-day football camp in Ypsilanti, Michigan, where he only attended three out of the five days due to a scheduling conflict. The time he was there was enough to earn him the MVP of this camp for outstanding leadership. He also attended the Detroit Lions football camp, which was also a five-day camp. There he earned the MVP award of the camp for all ages for outstanding leadership, which made us extremely proud as parents. These awards are all attributed to his hard work and holding himself to a high standard.

Most importantly, stay involved in what's going on with your child at school. Parents should know their son's teacher, go to conferences, and develop a relationship with the teacher so the child understands that academics are of the utmost importance and that you are an involved parent. Children should also understand the importance of academics and without good grades there will be no sports, free time, or games because academics are what's most important. We would advise parents to love their sons by hugging them and expressing their love to them in ways that make them feel cared for and appreciated. Even if a parent isn't in the home, whether it's the father or mother, go beyond what the courts might require. The money that's given will never be enough, so the time the parent spends with the child is what's most important. Be around your child more than anyone else could ever advise because no amount of money can replace or substitute for the quality time that a parent can and should be spending with their child.

The advice that we would offer to parents is to be honest with your children and not be afraid to let them know what the real world is like. Whether you have an only child or not, always let them know that it's okay to be an "outcast," from the standpoint of being a leader and doing things that others might not be doing or just doing things by themselves. This cuts down on youth running to gangs or other negative influences because they feel they need to be loved, wanted, or raised. Youth want discipline and structure, which is why they look up to and respect the coaches and mentors in their lives.

KEY POINTS FROM THIS CHAPTER

CHAPTER 9

REPORTING FROM THE FRONT ROW

ACTION STEPS AND ADVICE FROM THE NATION'S YOUTH LEADERS

CHAPTER 9

Throughout my career, I've witnessed the important role that the community and its leaders play in the lives of young men. They serve as mentors and help establish a network of civic groups, youth activities, and programs to provide our young men with safe havens they otherwise wouldn't have had. Below are a few of these individuals who have devoted their time to inspire and encourage our youth and whose efforts continue to make a difference. Many of their achievements can be used as a blueprint for creating new solutions to the ever-evolving issues faced by our young men today.

Joseph Radelet, Vice President of Mentoring Programs for Big Brothers Big Sisters of America: I believe young people need to be inspired. They need to know that there is reason for hope; they need to know that there are people working hard to make this a better place for the next generation. They need to know that there is a legacy being passed down to young people and that that legacy has to do with how we approach our education, families, neighborhoods, and how we rest on the shoulders of those who came before us to create a country where we can exercise our rights, freedoms, and responsibilities in ways that affect young people.

Mentoring at its core is how adults in our society care for our young, and at Big Brothers Big Sisters we have a formal mentoring process that enables adults to become mentors through our organization, based on our support structure and the training we provide them. Our support structure helps our mentors and mentees, or what we call our bigs and our littles, so that our youngsters are getting the support that they really need both in small ways and in large, informal and formal ways. This makes our society a strong society. In a neighborhood, a parent not only sees his or her youngsters as under their care, but if a youngster in their neighborhood is walking down the street, they provide a "hi," a wave, or some kind of care. And if a child is in trouble or in need of help, the entire neighborhood sees that child, watches over the children as they go to school, and expresses care for these children so they feel secure.

So what our agency is doing is involving adults who are mentoring in a formal way and who are giving examples, we hope, to our entire society that will increase a culture of caring toward children on the part of all adults. So if you are a college student who mentors, it means you care about youth. If you're in a fraternity and you mentor a child, this might be part of the requirements of the fraternity, but it still means you're going to take time to mentor a child. If you're a business employee, part of what you're doing is thinking about your customers and caring for them. And if you're a church member, you're saying the mission of my church is to follow in God's path and care for young people. It has to do with how we define who we are in our various roles throughout society as adults.

The success of mentoring depends on parents, and so there is really a four-legged stool here to make mentoring successful. The first is the volunteer Big Brother Big Sister, the second is the little brother or little sister, the third is the parent, and the fourth is Big Brother Big Sister staff. We need the dedication and involvement of all of those four groups to make mentoring successful. To apply this, I've been a big brother for the second time in my life myself, here in Philadelphia for the last nine years, to a youngster who is now eighteen and will be graduating from high school this spring. He comes from a family that's had a great deal of hardships. His grandmother has raised him, and I felt from the first time I met her that the reason my little brother bonded so well with me is because his lens on people and on relationships is through his grandmother. His mother died when he was quite young, and his father is incarcerated, and so his grandmother has been the influence of his life.

So first of all, a parent usually comes to us. Parents never come to us saying, "Fix my child," they come to us saying, "I am calling in all my chips from my community, all the possible resources on behalf of my child, and I can't do everything. I need a team member, somebody who is going to reinforce how I am raising my child." It's that initial invitation that is so important on the part of parents, and secondly, as big brothers and big sisters, we are resting on the shoulders of those parents, letting them know we are a team member with them. Our mission is to match the parent's goal for that child, connect with them, and support and assist in making the goal a reality.

From our perspective there are four R's, not three; we have reading, writing, and arithmetic, but the fourth R is relationships. If you talk with a teacher at length, they will talk about the value of their relationships with the children in their classroom. Without a good relationship, I can't really get through to that child. So what we emphasize to the teachers in our program is that relationships are the key.

Parents are the child's first teacher. Your relationship with your son is most important, and you along with the other parent are the most important guides for that child. No one can take that from you. Everybody else who has the welfare of that child in mind is a team member with you. As an organization, what I would say to parents is, how can we assist you? What can we do to help in this mentoring relationship? What can we do that will help you in the kinds of things that you're trying to work on with your child?

Secondly, I would say a mentor's role is to emphasize the positive. We are here to say to that child, you are a great person, you're fantastic, I didn't know you could do that. Our job as mentors is to reinforce the positive and be a part of the praise team for that child. So we ask parents what they are most proud of with their child and how they express that praise to their child. Many of us as parents understand that it's not easy to remember this on a day-to-day basis, especially when you've asked them four times to take the garbage out and they still haven't done it. However, we have to find ways to praise our children and keep them on the right path and let them know that nobody else is going to be like them and that nobody can ever be better than them at being who they are.

In the elementary setting, we should not underestimate the importance of what's going on in second, third, and fourth grade, in terms of the lifelong effects that these years have on youngsters. Boys tend to come along a little bit slower than girls, so boys need to find their niche, in terms of being recognized for what they're doing well. Teachers should give boys attention not just when they're doing something wrong, but praise them for positive things as well. The middle school grades are very important because young boys are trying to figure out everything from girls to who's going to be head of the pack to how to deal with bullies to cyberspace, even if the adults in their lives that they respect don't understand these problems. These young men are trying to sort out a lot, and the peer influence becomes even stronger. We have to become in tune to what they're wrestling with, and we have to let them know that we care about what they're wresting with and we care a lot more about it than whether they're sitting up straight in the classroom and not being disruptive. We care about them as people, and we see them as people who are going to have futures that are going to help us all.

Too many of our young men are going down a path that is resulting in this huge rate of incarceration. The rate of incarceration is affecting African American men and Hispanic men in particular. We have to recognize that this is a failure to our society. This is an omission in our society that we don't have time for these young men when they're in middle school and even before, because when we see the behaviors, we don't have time or say we don't have time. It's time to invest in these young people so when they get to be thirteen or fifteen they are not already incarcerated, and when they're eighteen to twenty-five, we're not having this incarceration rate that's so shameful for our society. We have better things to do with our money in this society than saying we're going to lock you up and throw away the key. Is that the best we have for our young people and young men? It can't be.

The task is evident in third or fourth grade, and focusing on winning back our boys is what we need to do as early as possible. Win them back to the legacy we want from them and recognize that it's hard work. It's not like passing a young person in a hallway and saying hi, then saying, now I'm a mentor to that child. Our youth have huge needs, and as a society, the question is whether we're going to be serious enough about caring for and connecting with our young people. We have to give the resources of our time and love to these young people because the end product has been prison. And the prison system doesn't have to be that way, but we have to decide that it's not going to be that way.

Iris K. Salters, President of the Michigan Educators Association: It's been proven that youth need adult role models. These adult role models need to be someone not only in the school setting, but also out of the school setting. It is so important especially for young men to have males in their environment that they can look to and be able to emulate in some ways. The other thing that's lacking is a sense of stability, especially with the economic situation facing families here in Michigan and across our nation. Children need that stability of knowing that you're going to continue to have a home; knowing that you're going to continue to have food, clothing, and other needs met in your environment; and feeling what that instability does to families.

Teachers can help in these situations by serving as adult role models in the school environment, which is key. The students' needs may be a smile, a pat on the back, or someone they can confide in and share their fears with. One thing that has concerned education for years is the lack of male role models, especially at the elementary grade levels. But certainly support staff has stepped into that responsibility. My husband was an elementary school maintenance and custodian worker. During that time, many of the young men followed him around and interacted with him. I say children need to be able to find this in their family life and community as well. By nature, the way education is structured, youth need a different instructor every year. With that it becomes harder to find that key role model for individuals. Schools have tried advisee groups to fill this void, where students are assigned to a person who's their educational mentor in that setting. Often those are not the match that's needed, so children need to be able to look out of that and find someone who can meet that requirement for them.

Teachers are facing a lack of stability in their environment. What that means is children are coming with more and more baggage because of the instability in their lives with our economic crisis. Many of our teachers are facing the same kinds of instability in their families. Students aren't coming ready to learn, not just in kindergarten, but even as you look at their daily expectations for the learning environment, many are coming without that good breakfast, without the number of hours of sleep they need; in essence, they are bringing community unrest with them, that then spills over into the environment. These are things for teachers that are very hard to make a difference with because many of them do not live in that community as such. There is also a real disconnect between what families think should be an investment of their time in education. Oftentimes in the surveys we've done, many families feel like homework is something that's an extra requirement on the family that may or may not be necessary. As educators, we know the extension of learning is key to the students retaining those concepts. So in some way, that idea of parent involvement must be understood in terms of what that means and figuring out how we can make a difference.

A community that is invested in the children—and not just their own children, but the student population in general—becomes the support for the teacher. Where a community is invested in the success of their children, you're not only going to have parents doing the kinds of things that you need to have done, but you're going to have a total community concerned about that and supportive of the educational environment, which is where we need to move to.

We have to reiterate that the success of the children, whether you're at the grandparent level or the parent level, directly impacts the success of your life. If we don't have productive individuals moving into the workforce, there is nobody to pay your Social Security or your retirement. So you have an investment not only in your children, but in the next generation of children to come. This is something we have to consistently remind ourselves of while figuring out the role of the community. A good place to start is with our faith-based community most of us grew up in, which became a support system for our children who went through it.

After having a young man myself, I understand that it's a day-to-day struggle. The one thing that we often discount in raising young boys is the idea of patience. You must have patience because students especially must go through certain times in their lives, and some of these times are very stressful on families. It's very important to have interaction and involvement in your children's lives. You need to know what they're doing and who their friends are, not so you can control every moment of their day, but so they know that you have that concern because you love them and want the best for them. You must also set expectations with young men and follow through with actions on these expectations. We also must make sure the follow-through is something that we can do and are willing to do, because most of the time, the follow-through causes hardship on the person who invoked the expectation.

My advice for teachers with male students is to go back to patience, in addition to making a special effort to build the trust, especially with minority males, because if they don't trust you, they don't give you a chance in the environment. Teachers who might not fit into the same minority group as these young men can be just as effective if they speak the truth and don't try and be anybody else but themselves. They may not be able to relate to these students in the same way that someone from their own minority group may be able to, but they need to interact with them from a place of honesty. The students need to know that the teachers care about them and that their caring is why they do what they do, and it doesn't mean that the boys have to emulate anyone else in the process.

Bobby Blount, NISD Board Trustee in San Antonio, Texas: Youth today need several things to be successful, one being the insight to obtain and achieve a vision. Not just a logistical vision of getting from point A to point B, but a vision of how they can be successful in the long run. As a part of establishing that vision, we have to give them opportunity to succeed in several different venues and expose them to different things. My vision may be narrow if all I see is very limited, but if youth are exposed to engineering, athletics, and other fields, that will open them up and expose them to things that will broaden their vision. The exposure they get from television and other things, they sort of mold themselves after that. To some degree, responsibility for this falls on adults, because if we don't expose them to more, how can we expect them to have a broader vision? Where the rubber meets the road is where we really have to provide opportunity for them.

They need opportunities to fail at things so they can learn and realize that you're going to fail in life, but that's what leads to more successes. The way that we give them opportunity is by exposing them to more things that assist them in becoming more well-rounded. If we want to give them an opportunity, we have to reinforce and provide them with an education. What I mean by that is not just the academic portion, which is very important. It's also important to give them the opportunity to become well-rounded so that they can achieve whatever they need, whether it's finances, mentoring, parental support, and everything else. It's very important for us to provide them with the skills necessary to be successful from various aspects. If youth want to go down a certain path or in a certain direction, we can help them go that way, but at the same time, we teach them that things change a lot and it's good to be prepared for other possibilities that might arise.

I've established a soccer club to create more exposure, because if I'm one who believes in expanding their vision, I must provide opportunities for them to do so. Soccer has become a very expensive sport, and the number of people playing has declined, so what our club has done is offer scholarships. We've gotten support from corporations to assist so that youth could still compete against those who could afford to pay the big money. We never want youth not to compete because of money, so what we've done is established ourselves as a corporation. My job is to be creative in finding funds so vision in young people can be established through opportunity.

I also work a lot with science bowls and have started something called the Texas for the race car event. I established this particular program because I wanted youth to have the opportunity to go through academics in the classroom but see the importance of how to apply it. That's important not only from an academic or educational standpoint, but it's also important to the youth. By providing more of a hands-on experience, children tend to become more interested and more involved. Principals have been shocked with the results with the youth who have gone through this program, from special education students to gang members.

One of the things I get fearful of in the different community organizations that I'm involved in is people who volunteer just to use the word volunteer, not realizing that you have to be just as committed as you would to your job if you're going to be successful. Young people pick up on this quickly, especially if you're there for weekend credit or just a way to feel good. Volunteers have to have the mindset that this is just as important to me as anything else, and by taking this approach, the young people will be much more receptive to you and success can be obtained. I also encourage the organizations that I work with to not accept mediocrity. The youth that come from the various organizations that I'm engaged with—I really want to teach them that they're going to be successful by making mistakes and learning.

Always have that high expectation of them and let them know you're going to push them to do their best. I also push the adults I work with as well because we need to model what we want out of our children. For an example, when we look at the achievement gap among students and see that numerical representation of the situation, that shouldn't be the threshold, the bar, or an excuse. The number is just a starting point. It's an opportunity that we need to look at, address, and fix and not treat it as a generalization or indictment of an entire system or process. We should recognize they may have a challenge, but let them become successful no matter who they are. As an organization, I always push that we have to do the very best we can, and when we talk about raising the bar, we have to make the bar as high as we can so that no matter who comes after us, they have to go over that same bar. We can't lower the bar by coming up with excuses like data and other things.

On our school district side, we had a program titled Making School More Family Friendly, to get more parent/guardian involvement. We did things from offering courses dedicated to specific parents' needs, to setting up parent night with different activities, to making visitors lots in the front of the school as opposed to administration parking, as a way to make it more inviting. We even included food as a means to get participation, which helped. When I delegate and establish different school committees, I usually try and get the parents engaged in whatever it may be, even if it's something I know I can do myself. This has been effective because asking parents for their input is a direct way to keep them involved with school activities.

Teachers can help students become successful by inspiring them and showing them how, by pushing them to do the very best they can, and, showing them they care, while gaining their trust. It's important for teachers to communicate that failure in the system isn't an option. You'll mess up, you'll make mistakes, but in the long run we want to make you the very best that you can be. A long-term plan and those types of things are great, but what happens with different youth is decided in a moment. Sometimes you have a student who might be struggling and you have the opportunity to ignore or help them, and that might have a longer-lasting impact than what people may think. If you lose out on moments, I can see how it might have a bigger impact over time than what people may realize. Another aspect related to teachers helping youth become successful is raising the bar for everyone. Some may assume that mediocrity for a student who's at a low level might be great, but that's not necessarily the case.

In the end, we want to be the very best we can, and maybe everybody doesn't make the top bar, but if you don't show the student that top bar, their focus may be on, why doesn't the teacher think I can achieve this—so their focus might be on the next bar instead of the top bar. Teachers should also communicate with everyone they possibly can, whether it's the parent, the guardian, the mentor, or that other teacher who might be involved in that child's life. It takes more than just the teacher to make that child successful, and the more communication that takes place, the more likely success will happen. Teachers should also have an interest in the whole child, not just from an academic standpoint. This can be done through knowing their other involvements and asking how they're doing in that part of their life as well.

Parents must set an example of how to be successful for their sons, showing them what a vision really is, what it means, and how to strive to achieve it, while encouraging them to stay focused on it no matter what. Even though the vision may change a bit later, it's important for them to see this example in their parents. It's also important for parents to support this vision; it's difficult dealing with young boys because some people confuse support with bonding. Bonding is good, but I'm referring to support in the sense of when they need to be somewhere, get them there. Even if you have a conflict with the young man being somewhere or have to go to a party of some sort, you should support him in what he's doing. It's extremely important for us to be there for them and set that good example.

Advice that I have for teachers is just to make sure they don't have any stereotypes about male students. Data shows information about the male student—so be it, but what's important is treating each one as an individual before you. The data is never 100 percent anyway, so we should assist each student in becoming successful in what they need to do, no matter what. This is critical, because people oftentimes give a reason in the form of an excuse as to why someone can't do something or shouldn't be able to do something, without ever getting the chance to. Teachers should also, when possible, make themselves available when students are in need or ask for help. If they go to that one teacher for help and they're rejected, they may never ask someone else in the future, and in the long run asking for help never paid off.

Steven Huerta, President of All of Us or None, Texas: Young people today need more focused curricula related to life skills. They need to learn about emotional and intellectual intelligence, and they need more courses to equip them to deal with the many variables that they have to deal with, including mass media, music, and the different influences that often lead to the use of drugs and alcohol, among other things. They need more social interactive skills being taught in schools as well as by parents in order to be prepared not only for the workforce, but for life itself. Most importantly, what they need is two-parent involvement. Not two parents in the home necessarily, but two parents actively involved in their lives. Their parents can be in two separate households, but collectively working together for the betterment of the child involved. Even though it's difficult at times for parents in separate households to get along, it's accomplishable, especially when the parents aren't focused on themselves, but on what's best for that child. This is more attainable when each approach and interaction among the parents is tailored toward the overall plan and objective of what they want to produce in the future of that young person.

Each father that I come in contact with, as well as some mothers, comes from a single-parent home. These single-parent homes exist as a result of separation, divorce, or incarceration, among other things. Mainly, the fathers aren't around, nor a male role model or provider who could pick up the slack to teach certain life skills. So what we do is teach the concept of parenting to them, seeing that they never really saw or experienced it themselves. Oftentimes some of the issues we face, we keep them locked away in the closet doors of our minds, and the right person comes along with the key to open it up and help us realize it's been there all the time. So what we like to do is unlock that door for them and allow them to realize what they really want for their children, while assisting them to accomplish it.

The behaviors that teachers expect in the classroom can't be blanket. The rules can be blanket, but the behavioral expectations can't. Most of our teachers are females, and many of them tend to expect the same behavior out of all the students. However, young boys are different, and oftentimes their rough play and interaction is interpreted as bullying or disruptive of some sort. This isn't to say that these actions aren't there, but many instances it's taken a little too far. It's key for teachers to have good relationships with their students, and doing so provides the teacher with a better understanding of such behaviors and if they are cause for the attention that they're now receiving. Another thing that needs to be considered is when the child does something wrong, the mom is usually the one that receives a call from the school. So many fathers are unaware of what's taking place in their child's lives, whether it's rewards or disciplinary punishment. So I always encourage teachers to give a call to both parents.

Teachers should challenge our youth, and challenge them to reach every level that they possibly can. Take negative energy that young men might be expressing and find that niche within that student and turn it into a positive, and watch it grow. Allow them to express themselves and relieve frustrations that may be causing behavioral problems in school, in your classroom, under your supervision, in a positive light. Have them be leaders; maybe once a week rotate and let them be leaders, because they need to obtain positive leadership positions at every chance possible.

One of my colleagues and very good friends told me that I was a rag man. If you think about it, every rag that we see at one point belonged to something—something beautiful, something whole, and somewhere down the line someone thought that rag was no longer any good and they threw it away. What I try to do is pick up that rag and put it back together and make it whole again. As people keep throwing away rags, I will continue picking them up, which is connected to every life that I come in contact with, even those that others might see as a rag that should be thrown away because it has no use. I pick it up and connect it to what it was originally a part of, which is the connection that many young boys desire.

Dee James, Executive Director of Mansions Day School, Columbus, Ohio: Young people need two things, one being highly qualified people to teach them and care about them, and the other being discipline. I think we're lacking in both. We have people who are very well educated, and they do a good job teaching, but we really need to go back to the old-fashioned way of people being concerned about the students they teach. I think also a disciplined environment is missing, not the kind of discipline where people are spanked or receive corporal punishment, but discipline where they understand what the boundaries and parameters are for them to work in. Most children today don't have people who do that, and most children are confused as to where to stop. So they push the envelope, and that takes the education out of the classroom because behavioral issues are the focus. This lends itself to children in first, second, third grade being labeled as having behavioral issues because the foundation wasn't set early on as to what the expectation was for them.

Our school meets these needs because first, I hire people who love my children. I look for people who exude the spirit of what I'm looking for in this school, which is a nurturing and caring concern for children as well as being able to reach them and discipline them. When teachers walk into a class the first day, the students should know what is expected from them. This usually cuts off any kind of negative behavior because children are going to be children, and they're going to play if they can play, and they're going to talk if they can talk. We express to children that when it's time to study it's time to study, and when it's time to play it's time to play, and we do both with vigor. The way we do it is by hiring people who like children.

Teachers have to feel that it's because of the nurturing and caring environment of the school that the children do as well as they do. Our children here know that they are loved. I know there is a new movement taking place where children aren't to be touched because of the negative media attention. However, I hire people who can touch children, who can hug children, who can affirm children, because I think that a child who is affirmed, loved, and nurtured will give you his best. Children are natural adult pleasers; they want to please adults, and they want to make us happy. Making us happy might mean that you're not an A student, but you're going to give me your best effort. We give effort grades here, up to fourth grade, because we want to teach our children that a strong work ethic will produce the grades you want. We feel that strong work ethic will carry them into adulthood, so they're not temped to cheat for that A or B when they become tenth-graders. It will already be understood that hard work is the way that you have to do it. So in essence, I only hire people who fit into the mission of this school.

Parent involvement is 100 percent, based on our expectations of them as well as the fact that I only accept those who fit into the mission of the school, just as the teachers. The reality is we expect parents to be involved, and the level of education we strive for is necessary for parental involvement in order for the child to see the level of success that is expected of them. We don't want parents to become overly involved with the homework because we want to make sure that the child knows it, but we do expect the parents to have a place in the home where the child can do his homework in the same place consistently every day. Children need expectations, but they also need to be supported, which is missing in today's education.

I grew up poor in the state of Georgia. My parents were uneducated people, but the reality was they expected me to do better than they did. They expected me to go farther than they went, and that's what we tell our children here. It doesn't matter if your father is a doctor, lawyer, or an engineer, we expect you to outpace your parents with integrity and character in place. Our children are go-getters because that's what they see and that's what's expected of them. I've seen that if you expect a little bit from children they will give you a little bit, and if you expect them to reach for the sky, they may only get to the treetop, but they're reaching for the sky. Success happens here because we expect them to be successful, and parents are involved because they know our expectations, which happens to be theirs as well. They're happy to have a school and a school head that is an extension of the thinking that they have for their own children, which is what's missing in schools across the country. The expectation level is too low, and the nurturing and caring is not there, and the parents are not involved enough.

There has to be a parent-school relationship in order for that child to be successful. It's very difficult to do one without the other.

Schools must have some type of program that involves parents. They need to awaken the interest of parents and let them know that their child cannot be successful without them or whoever the caregiver is. What has worked for us is hosting spaghetti dinners in the evening for parents, where they can come and discuss different topics that are important for them. We have different speakers come in and talk with our parents, and this has been effective in keeping parents involved. Many of the parents are able to provide this service, and cost may be minimal, if anything. We've had talks on health and fitness and college. You have to put in place some kind of program that deals with parents outside of education, because if you don't do that, parents are not educated on understanding why it's important for them to be involved.

Most of us who are educated understand this, and that's why I think doctors' children becomes doctors and lawyers become lawyers, because their parents are able to tell them, show them, and model for them. If you have children who don't have these types of role models, how are they going to get to that level or get anywhere close to it if someone is not taking the time to help the parents or caregivers understand the importance of helping their children become better individuals than they are. I think it's problematic that there aren't programs in place to educate parents. And there has to be some kind of incentive in it, and I think it's just the fact that most parents would like to see their children do well. We have people who speak with our boys and girls about character, integrity, and respect for themselves and others.

We have Merrill Lynch coming in for our section on economics to teach our students about money and what to do with it, while getting our parents involved in understanding economics—teaching the importance of credit, understanding investments, the importance of savings, and the importance of not spending all the money that comes through your hands on stuff.

I have a fifteen-year-old and a twenty-one-year-old, and my twenty-one-year-old is a senior at Morehouse College in Atlanta. He has a 3.6 GPA and is receiving all kinds of awards there for his diligence. My youngest son is a 4.0 student in advanced classes, and I marvel sometimes at their ability to do what they do. My husband and I are so grateful to God for keeping them the way they are now and keeping them in the belief of what we've taught them regarding their integrity, character, and learning what's right and doing it. They got the work ethic, which started here by setting that stage for success by providing an environment where they can consistently come every day to do their work, in their space, at their desk. We also taught them that the pride of doing well comes from within, and parents need to teach their children not to look to the outside for praise for doing what should be expected.

We expected our children to do well. We didn't pay our kids for As, but we might go out to dinner as a family to celebrate them. Paying for As is not necessarily a bad thing, and every family has their own way of doing things, but I personally think good grades should be expected of our children; that's their job. Parents' jobs might be to go out and make money, but the children's job is to go to school and do their best. My children are not perfect, but they knew what was expected of them.

Another issue is we aren't teaching young men how to be men. A woman can't teach a man how to be a man; that's a man's job. Unfortunately, many of the homes are headed by women, so we need men to step up, whether it is big brothers, uncles, or a grandpa. But that boy by the time he gets to twelve or sixteen is in dire need of male examples. If there is no family member, it's key for boys to somehow get involved with a positive male role model in their lives. Parents need to also support their boys and understand that somewhere around the second and third grade, even though it hasn't been fully documented, that boys can't sit still as well, and they don't focus as well, and it's not the time for that paintbrush approach that they're all ADD so let's put them on Ritalin.

Boys need to be told: sit down right now, this is not a democracy, I'm in charge, and you will do what I tell you to do, so sit. Our children need that, regardless to what race they are; they need someone to say I'm in charge and you're not, and I need you to do what I asked you to do. They also need love, discipline, direction, and they need a role model. They need to know that someone cares about them; they need someone just to say "I am so very proud of you." The children at my school get a big kick out of me telling them I'm proud of them and reaffirming them. Parents also have to listen to their children, because children want someone to talk to, and if you aren't there to listen, they're going to talk to their peers or someone else, who perhaps might give advice that you would not. There have been many times my sons have told me things where I had to bite my tongue because I wanted to respond.

I understood that they needed to talk it out, they needed to talk it through, they don't always want you to give them a solution, and they at times just want you to listen. The connection with that is patience and love, and if you're doing it right, children will know that they're accepted. I heard Charles Stanley say almost twenty years ago that children need ABCs. They need to be approved of; they want someone to approve of who they are and what they're doing. The B is they need to belong, and usually it's the family that provides this first, but in this school, the children know that they are wanted, loved, and that they belong to the body, because we call ourselves a family. So if something is wrong with one of the students here, most of us are all involved in it. The C part is that children need to feel that they are competent at something.

One of the problems is that when America looks at the fourth-grade literacy rate, they determine how many prisons they're going to build in the future. One of the problems is that we miss the opportunity for our children to be successful if the early intervention in education is not there. Because if you can't read in America, you're pretty much destined not to be a success, and that's unfortunate. A child who feels incompetent is a child who feels no hope. And if you feel no hope, then why do anything; I'm not going anywhere, nobody expects anything of me, and nobody cares if I succeed. Then enters the opportunity for negative behavior, gang involvement, and other things that make you feel you don't belong and that you're not a part of a group or family.

Jay Dewispelaere, President/CEO of Pride Youth Programs: Youth need positive role models in their lives—someone who's going to give them time—parents, maybe a teacher, coach, or just a friend. This is probably one of the most important things they need. If we can give them the proper guidance, then they're able to live a healthy lifestyle that will keep them away from drugs and alcohol. It's been the key in my life as well as in hundreds of thousands of families that I've worked with across the country.

Our organization meets these needs by allowing youth to belong to something bigger. The majority of the thousands of youth who are a part of Pride Youth Programs have chosen that lifestyle for whatever reason. Usually most of them have a story, and that story consists of a family member who is involved with drugs and alcohol, or they've lost a friend to drunk driving, or whatever the case might be. Our organization helps them to belong to something bigger. From visiting youth all over the country, the one thing that I have found is they don't feel they have credibility in their own community. If they choose this drug- and alcohol-free lifestyle, many of their friends might make fun of them, so we give them an organization that is bigger than their local group, which makes them feel like there are thousands of youth like them and it's okay to be drug and alcohol free.

What got me involved in Pride Youth Programs was reading a survey that asked who students go to when they have a question about drugs and alcohol. Over 75 percent of the students said they go to their friends. From that point on, it just made sense for me to work with youth, which I've been doing my whole life anyway. What that comes back to is youth teaching each other that peer-to-peer relationship that we support and foster, which sets us apart from other youth programs.

Parent involvement is probably the most successful part of our program. We have a parent action team, and we teach how to involve parents without overwhelming them and showing them different ways to communicate with their children. Even the youth in our program who are models around the country in terms of helping children avoid drugs and alcohol have difficulty at times communicating with their parents. Even great young people who go off to college and have successful careers have difficulty communicating with their parents. I'm a father of five. We've adopted two other children, and we've raised other children besides that, and our household is always full of children. However, I can still tell you that it's difficult for even me to communicate. It's not so hard as my children grow older, but getting them through those formative years can be very difficult. And I can't communicate to parents enough that their child doesn't need another friend in their lives. They have plenty of friends; they need a parent, and parents must separate themselves from the idea of being their child's friend.

I was at the White House once because the first lady, Laura Bush, was focusing on helping young adult males. She and I had this discussion about how even her children weren't exempt from using drugs and alcohol, nor were mine. I'm certainly not comparing myself to the Bush family, but if their children aren't exempt, why should anybody think theirs are? Parents have to support their children by being their parent and not their friend. When they do something wrong, dust them off and be there for them. In doing so, move forward and don't get hung up on the past because they'll keep seeing a continuation of failure that way.

If you are engaging youth in a successful program that is purely from the heart, the parents will come. Even the worst parents want to be a good parent. Whoever you or I classify as the worst parent, they want to be a good parent, even if they've made multiple mistakes in their lives. If you offer a quality program with meaningful results, you'll get the parents involved. Something that is so underrated is just asking parents to get involved. However, there is a fine line between getting parents involved without parents coming in and trying to take over. We've developed over the years a good model that has worked by giving them something meaningful to do, and be a part of, while feeling like they're participating in a way that's not overwhelming the child. Because the young people don't come to the program to spend time with their parents, they're coming there to get away from them. It's important that parents feel that the time they're spending is worthwhile, and we make sure it's recognized in a way that is fulfilling to the parent doing the work but isn't alienating the other parents in the group.

I can walk into a school building and tell you within five minutes the attitude and mindset of that school district. It's going to start first in that building with the principal and that principal's attitude, which now breaks down to the teacher. If you show me a great school building, even if that master principal is in there making it work, they also have master teachers that are making it work. I always start with the principals for support, but then go to the master teachers to really understand what's going on. What we should have is more mentoring going on in these buildings today—master teachers working with the younger teachers or, if you will, the problem teachers, trying to bring their attitude back on board, and more importantly, showing them how they can become more successful. There will always be negative people in every industry, but you have to focus on the positive and not the negative. Many of the teachers who can make this change were more than likely motivated by a teacher in their lives, and they have a lot to offer the new teachers, who can use their experience to be successful.

Teachers should never back down from their students and should always set boundaries and rules in the classroom. In doing so, show that you, the teacher, care, and never be afraid of asking for help from a more experienced teacher that appears to be having more success. Their job is to educate that male student in the classroom, and some make it very difficult to do that, but don't give up on them. Hold your ground and manage your classroom, and most of the students will comply with what you expect. Teachers should also put life lessons into their teaching to make it more meaningful. I'm not good at algebra, but I would probably know a lot more about algebra if my teacher had creatively used life lessons to teach it. If teachers are prepared and organized, they will be successful and have the greatest chance of helping students succeed.

Rich Dutra-St.John, Co-founder of Challenge Day, which was featured on *The Oprah Winfrey Show*: Challenge day started because twenty-one years ago, my wife and I decided that we didn't want our children to go through some of the teasing, separation, isolating, and bullying that we did in school. So we came up with this idea that if we could demonstrate the love and connection that are actually possible in our schools, then in fact we could change things. We wanted to show young people that love, compassion, and acceptance can actually take place in our schools. What we saw is that young people need to be celebrated, have someone believe in what they are capable of doing, give them a way to do that, and celebrate them in the process. Whether that's the teacher at schools, or the parents at home, or their peers, they need to have the freedom to be and the understanding that they're good enough just the way they are. So what we do in one day is show that that's actually a possibility.

On "challenge" day we start out with icebreakers and activities that allow people to mix and get to know people that they normally wouldn't have talked to. We encourage them to actually reach out to the one who seems most different on the outside so they can get to know them on the inside. In terms of the resistance, what happens is we just believe and see them as being totally capable of coming together. So over the course of the day, slowly but surely you can feel the ice melt on the resistant people, and we lead up to an activity called the power shuffle. This is when everyone lines up on one side of the room, and we call out different categories, different forms of oppression, and if they have experienced that in their life, they cross over the line. This way they get to see that everybody crosses that line at some point. Nobody likes it, so why hurt each other over differences. This is a really powerful activity, and what people get to see is that they're not alone. It gets really emotional, and people get vulnerable, and in that place of vulnerability, compassion happens.

We're able to be successful in breaking down barriers in such a short time because we're not asking anybody to do something that we wouldn't do. So we walk into a room of a bunch of strangers who have no idea who we are, and we role model from our experiences and hearts and give them permission to do the same. The power of the work is that we all want the same thing, but behind it all we believe that every person on the planet wants to be celebrated for who they are. So we do what's called look for the light—look for the brilliance in each person and assume the best. We give them an excuse to be the human beings that we know they are.

We encourage adults and parents to participate in these events because we know that the youth need support, which is one of our goals. We often ask them to raise their hand if they remember half of what they learned in school, and nobody raises their hand. So we ask, "What about 25 percent," and finally about a quarter of the people raise their hand. Next, we say, "Raise your hand if you remember the adults in your life who loved you, supported you, who believed in you," and they all raised their hands. So the most important thing we can do as parents, teachers, and community members is show these young people that we really care about them. This is how we involve and invite parents to come, and we usually have one adult for every six students in the room.

Before we go, we ask that every school have a "Be the Change" team, which includes parents, teachers, and community members, and the students on the campus. They, as a group, decide what are the goals, why do we want a challenge day, what are we trying to accomplish here. After challenge day, that group gets together and continues to do whatever follow-ups are taking place on campus in conjunction with our office and the different circles of change we have across the country. They come up with their plans and figure out how they're going to put them in practice.

During our events, we coach adults on how to be allies for the young people and what to expect during these events. We also encourage them to reach out to those they judge the most or have the most difficulty with so they can get to know them on the inside instead of judging who they think they are on the outside. We give them tips on confidentiality and how to deal with sensitive issues. At the end of the challenge day, we meet with the adults who were present, just to make sure that no young people fall through the cracks. They give us feedback, and we always have a counselor who can take issues and address them right on the spot.

Teachers can help youth become successful by finding out what's important to them and helping them achieve their dream. I have a friend who wrote a book called No More Turning Away. He was an educator at all different levels, and he had a 100 percent graduation rate from a continuation school for all the students who had been kicked out of the system. What he said is, you can teach a child to read a phone book in a dark closet if they knew it was for them—such is the power of a dream. So it's important for teachers to find out what their students' dreams are. When I was a teacher, I had students write their autobiographies and tell me their dreams. What I would do is go home and look up stories and articles that had to do with each student's dreams. I would share it with them and let them know that I supported them in their dreams, and after thirty days, we developed special relationships after sharing with all the students. Even if someone gets smart and says they want to be a drug dealer, well let's show them how math is going to help them be a drug dealer. While this may seem odd at first, you must connect with a boy where he is right now, only then can he dream bigger dreams. Whatever their dream is, show how the subject matter or the thing you're trying to teach them is going to help them get their dream. This is the answer to how teachers can help youth become successful.

Parents need to give young boys permission to feel their heart. Boys are often told there are only a few emotions that they can have; they can be angry or they can be funny. This creates separation and harshness, and it's like they can only settle for that type of connection. And we all feel things, so it's key for parents to let their sons feel their heart and let them know that real men can stand in all of who they are.

Teachers need to notice and appreciate students for their individual gifts, appreciate their hearts for their participation, and, if they know what their dreams are, support them and let them know they're cared about. In doing so, instantly they have an ally. Young people want to be seen, heard, and celebrated, and they want to do their best, even if we don't think it. For me it means looking them in the eyes, it means stopping and making contact in whatever ways are appropriate for that relationship, it means finding out what's important to them and helping them have that.

If I could change one thing on the planet, especially when it comes to boys, it would be for young boys and men to understand that it's a gift to be a young boy and a man, and the only way we can experience the fullness of our gift is if we celebrate it for that special gift that we have. Whether we're strong, physically gifted, or emotionally gifted, each individual should be seen and celebrated for who he is. I once thought that all of the men I met that were exceptional were exceptional men. Now I'm understanding that every man is exceptional if we put our energy into getting to know that about him.

KEY POINTS FROM THIS CHAPTER

CHAPTER 10

THE ULTIMATE GAME PLAN

CHAPTER 10

One of the hardest jobs young men face is learning good manners and respect when they haven't seen it demonstrated or received it themselves. They need to be taught by example that good decisions can keep you where bad choices can't take you. This can only be understood through demonstration by a loving and caring adult. Seeing the manifestation of these values will give young men the affirmation they need to internalize the values in their own lives, because if they can change the way they see a situation, the reality of that vision will automatically change how they act in it. Caring adults should relate to and try to understand youth as best as they can because in order to effectively help someone, you must know their wants before you can successfully address their needs.

In my communication workshops, I show adults exactly how to address the wants and needs of young people. Regardless of what an adult's intention is, if he can't determine the need of a young person, he can never effectively help that young person. To reach optimum impact, adults have to prove to that young person that they understand him and they can identify with what's important to him. This is key, because most young people have a degree of selfishness. They're not concerned with anything besides their wants and needs. Therefore, adults must strategically appeal to their selfish side in order to prove that they have their best interest at heart. This is one of many strategies that I teach adults in my live events.

The greatest gifts that can be given to young men are love, security, faith, time, and encouragement. Equally important, they should be given the ability to dream and be taught to believe in themselves. They need to know that if they fail, they have a support system to encourage and not criticize them. They're desperate for someone to help them get through life's toughest problems and reach victory. Showing them compassion, hope, support, and positive reinforcement will encourage young men tremendously in becoming all they were created to be. To assist in building their self-esteem, they need to have as many small victories as possible. This plays a vital role in their development because the greatest fear males have, young or old, is failure. They expect to win repeated victories in every aspect of their lives. Success to them becomes second nature only after they've experienced it firsthand a number of times.

Great men are defined by what they've done and what they've overcome in the process. Teaching and modeling these concepts to young men will help this generation of youth live for a purpose, to impart a positive, lasting influence on the world that will stand long after they're gone. We must embrace the opportunity and obligation of teaching them that they are the next best models, because they are the newest generation. All other generations before them were examples of what to do and what not to do in order to maximize their lives.

Let's think in terms of cars for a moment. Every year, a new model comes out, and it's expected to be better than the previous year's model because it was created by a team that was mindful of the flaws as well as the positive attributes of the previous model. Our young men are just like updated cars. The only difference is cars have higher expectations placed on them than are placed on today's young men.

If we had negative or mediocre expectations of the cars we build, they would need repairing much sooner than warranted by normal wear. In the same regard, males face several obstacles and challenges because of the low expectations placed on them. They're often set up just like cars that need repairing because they weren't built properly. As stated in the parenting chapter, "it's better to build a child than to repair an adult." What we're facing is a generation of young men that need repairing even before they become adults due to the lack of proper building on their foundation. This is evident in the differences we see between boys and girls. In countless aspects of life, society doesn't have the same expectations for young men as it does for young women. A few major examples include who's expected to fail and succeed in our school systems, who's more likely to be irresponsible, and who's more likely to have run-ins with the law. There's also an expectation of girls having more self-control regarding sex than our young men. These are just a few of the direct correlations to boys having higher rates of homicide, suicide, assault, burglary, and rape; school dropouts, school suspensions, school expulsions, juvenile detainment, and incarceration return.

Along with the high expectations, it's critical for young men to have others instill in them that they're valuable, special, and powerful. They need to know that every day above ground is a great one that comes with a vast amount of opportunity that is directly assigned to them. When this message is communicated with love and respect, we might in years to come be reading their books or attending their workshops to help save someone else's life. This is realistic because this is how things happened in my life. As one who was heading down the wrong path, I'm fully aware that death or incarceration could have easily been my reality and changed the entire course of my life. All young men who have been labeled or have done something wrong and committed violent acts can do anything they put their minds to when given the right opportunity.

Without the help of others and the right opportunity, I wouldn't have graduated from high school, gone on to play college football, and graduated from college, and I surely would not have become a national speaker. I am troubled sometimes by wondering, "Would many of the people who assisted me have done so if they had known the difficulties I had faced?" There's no way of knowing, but we can't deny that young men are often labeled by what they've done instead of who they are and what they are capable of doing. Many aren't given the opportunity to prove themselves to be anything different, based on the mistakes that they've made. Take the little boy who gets his name on the board for misbehaving. In most cases, there's nothing he can do to get it taken off. In his eyes, he sees no real value in correcting his behavior because he doesn't see that it's going to make a difference. So, he often does something else by the end of class to draw negative attention to himself because he's not given an opportunity to prove otherwise.

The major concern with issuing punishment in hopes of correcting behavior is that when the behavior stops, the old behavior will resurface if an alternative behavior is not reinforced. To effectively assist young men in excelling, the greatest asset you can give them is an incentive that's meaningful and the ability to change their mindset. If we only get them to change their behavior, they won't understand why they made the change, which places them at risk of returning back to the same behavior as before. When young men understand that they have an important role to play, it reveals why certain behaviors are relevant. It's often effective simply to reinforce to youth that they are needed. That creates a positive environment and enables a teacher to recognize and intervene in problems before they occur. Many young men who are asked for help will willingly give it and view being asked as a compliment. They often open up and become more vulnerable because the small responsibility that was given to them was enough to communicate that the adult trusted them with an important job.

Young boys have a burning desire to receive positive attention, especially from an older male—someone they view as strong, powerful, and confident, who can instruct them in becoming the same. If they aren't exposed to these types of men as their teachers, they need to make contact with them outside of school. Interacting with normal people who do what they would like to do or who are how they would like to be is a turning point in every young man's life. Connecting these young men with older, positive males who believe in them and treat them with respect is ideal because the young men long for positive attention. Most of the time when people see young boys by themselves or in a group, they look away in fear of being threatened in some way. When society identifies these boys as positive men, major change will take place. People will begin to feel safe again because these young men won't feel like outcasts in their own communities and thus look angry. They will be received and acknowledged as part of the community and not just a threat to it.

Males feel secure when they know they have a place in society that's safe and dedicated to them. The opposite is true when all they see is what they have been told that they can achieve and where they fit because they still feel that others don't understand them. Most of what others see is on the surface: their actions, but not the cause of their actions, which is never recognized. A young boy who starts a fight with another boy might do so because he's jealous of the relationship the other young man has with his father. On the surface, it might appear that he doesn't like the young man and wants to get revenge, when actually the fight could have taken place with anyone who reminded him of the pain he feels about his relationship with his father.

Conflict like this could be avoided if adults recognized what certain behaviors meant and then took the correct action. Whenever anyone is addressing issues with young men, they should do so in small steps. In general, males respond better to fewer questions than more. They may give less information than you want, but that's as much as they can give at one time. The most ineffective ways to address them are lecturing or interrogating them. How you communicate information determines a great deal of how engaged they will be to receive it.

This chapter will include several suggestions for ensuring the success of our young men. The first step toward success starts at home, so I will begin with parents. Parents of boys must understand that their child is visually stimulated, so teaching to this learning style will provide maximum results. When boys make wrong choices, it's a good idea to have them draw the situation on paper and point out where they could have made a better decision. This works mainly in homes where the parents have a good relationship with the child and frequently model the behavior they want to see out of their children.

Another great strategy parents can use to teach their children about decision-making is by reading the newspaper with them. Newspapers are catalogs of decisions that people have made, along with their results, whether good or bad. You can show your child how a person sentenced to jail time made a decision along the way that resulted in an undesirable punishment. It can also be a reality check to review the obituary column with them for young men who are the same age as they are and who were involved in the same things they are involved in. This technique is much more effective than watching the news because it provides fewer distractions and the parents or adults are better able to control the interpretation of the story.

This same strategy with the newspaper can be applied to the positive things that young people are doing as well, even though they're rarely publicized. Showing young people the positive accomplishments that their peers accomplished as a result of choices they've made is also an encouraging way to show your children what's possible. The best time for parents to speak with their sons is when they are tired, relaxed, excited, or happy about something out of the ordinary. During these times, the boys' focus is not on withholding information or determining the possible motive behind the discussion, but on the situation at hand.

Parents must also consider their sons' education. Parents send their children to school to learn and place sole responsibility on the teacher for teaching them, which should never be the case. Teaching should be a joint effort from the parent and teacher. Parents should know what's being taught to their children and reinforce it at home, especially if they agree. As a parent myself, I understand that I might not agree with certain things my children learn at school. Moreover, the schools might not teach them some things they need to know.

How I've assisted in my children's learning process is by incorporating in their daily activities what I think is important for them to learn. For instance, I don't allow my children to watch much TV, but when they do, I sometimes watch it with them. I do this to monitor what they're watching but also to seek teaching moments. During commercials, I'll have them write down a few new words they're not familiar with and have them find the meanings. You can offer various incentives to challenge them further or make it into a game of some sort, depending on the child. This helps in developing their vocabulary as well as listening skills, both of which are challenges that most young boys face. They can also learn about character and choices by being introduced to certain nonfiction books or magazines showing them people who've been successful or unsuccessful as a result of their decisions. Youth can really appreciate this because it's a real-life situation, not something fabricated to coerce them into making good decisions.

Poor communication is the barrier that stands between parents and children getting and receiving good information. I'm a firm believer in the power of effective communication and what it does for relationships. After my workshops, I'm frequently approached by parents and teachers thanking me for teaching them basic strategies that will immediately improve how they interact with youth. I commonly hear from adults how they're now able to relate to youth from all walks of life as a result of learning the four elements of communication and understanding the two ways communication is interpreted. These two elements of communication alone are responsible for several success stories between teachers and students who once had conflicts.

Also, specific to young males, I teach why it's important to tell them what you want instead of what you don't want. The word "don't" doesn't register in the subconscious mind.[2] For instance, if I said, "You don't see an orange cat barking," your mind picks up on "orange cat barking." This is exactly how young people receive information that they're told not to do. Thus, it's important for boys to receive direct instead of indirect instructions and information.

When I was a young boy, my mother would tell me "Don't do this" or "Don't do that," and I would do exactly what she said not to do. Why? Because she was indirectly instructing me, and all the information wasn't getting through the mental filters. I would get frustrated with myself because I could hear what she said, but it just didn't register. After hearing what she said, before I knew it I was doing the exact opposite. When she mentioned that she had told me not to do something, I would ask myself, "Why did you do that after she just told you not to?" When adults miscommunicate like this, in most cases the boys start to identify themselves as being unable to follow instructions. Parents can assist their sons as well as raise their own level of consciousness by having their sons keep track of how many times they say the word "don't," and giving their sons an incentive/reward for each time they record the word. This activity can keep parents aware of how to give instructions to their sons as well as enhance the children's communication and listening skills in the process.

Since parents and caregivers need to be aware of their children's academic performance, it's in the children's best interest for their parents to have a good relationship with their teachers. This lets teachers know parents have a genuine concern for their child and expect the teachers to as well. The way students are treated has a direct impact on how involved the parents are at school, specifically with teachers. Even if parents aren't able to meet with teachers, it's good to make a phone call or, better yet, send an e-mail. Sometimes written communication is the best method. When parents are talking with teachers about an issue regarding their child, in many cases the teachers might not be listening to what's being said because they're processing a response. This is especially true when teachers feel as though they are being attacked. Letters are an excellent means to mutual accountability because each response can be documented and utilized as a future reference. Letters also communicate to teachers that you've invested a portion of time into the overall advancement of your child and you are a concerned parent, even when you can't be there physically.

Students who are high academic achievers often attend schools that create different positive ways for parents and teachers to interact. These types of relationships encourage teachers to set high expectations and assist students in obtaining excellence, even if it means making alternative education accessible to those who might need it. Parents involved in an interactive atmosphere support teachers in the areas of academics and discipline to create a successful accountability system for the student. Together, parents and teachers provide a variety of discipline strategies that are more focused on each young person, as opposed to one single tactic that may not work for every student. Teachers sometimes make the mistake of doing things one way, especially when they aren't getting parental support, and expecting everyone to conform to that style.

In my teaching career, I've seen things done and done things that were both right and wrong, but I have learned from them all. The most intriguing aspect of my teaching career was learning how much more effective male teachers could be with male students. The phenomenon is amazingly consistent across the board, regardless of race or socioeconomic status. Whenever male students have male teachers who are firm and loving and show their genuine care for each student, success is almost guaranteed. However, female teachers are and can be effective as well, especially when they utilize approaches that specifically meet the needs of young boys. One strategy is to ask their students what they want to do for a profession. They can then start calling them by their career title, but explain that their career doesn't define them; they define their career. It's amazing what it does to their behavior when you instill this truth in their belief system.

The greatest need that all males have, young or old, is respect, and when this need is met, their behavior can be controlled by whoever is meeting this need. In conjunction with addressing the students respectfully, teachers should put their students' pictures on the classroom wall, as they do for famous people who have made their marks in history. Students should learn that these people all overcame adversity to achieve their success and have become examples for them to follow. This has the power to instill in the students that no one has ever been defeated until they accept defeat as a reality. In my home, we have a "wall of fame," on which, as a reward, my children can place a picture either of themselves or one that they've drawn. They can achieve this by completing a number of tasks that are realistic for them to accomplish. It's important to make sure obtaining a position on the wall is achievable, because if it's something out of their reach, failing to achieve it can cause more harm than good. The intent is to teach them that if they give life their best, they can and should expect to become a person of influence. This message is exactly what teachers should be communicating to students.

Educators can begin or proceed with this process by keeping young men involved in the learning environment. Give them the chance to assist and possibly lead a section of a lesson to show that they understand and are part of the learning process, but only when you're certain that they're capable. If young men are put in situations where they're likely to fail, they may become unruly toward the teacher and/or the students. Be sure that classwork and homework are applicable to the everyday situations they see and experience.

In order to hold their interest, the curriculum they learn from should also be male friendly. It should consist of activities that also meet and cater to the needs of the visual learner. Teachers should also form relationships with their students by building rapport, which is done by allowing them to have as many small victories as possible and being respectful of their perspectives. Letting them pass out materials and even make academic suggestions when possible can be great ways for teachers to build rapport and express their trust in these students. Young men also appreciate when you allow yourself to be vulnerable to a certain degree without losing credibility and letting them know you're not perfect. At the foundation of my success in speaking to youth around the country has been sharing stories about my life's successes and failures. It breaks down their defenses and answers the question on many of their minds: "How do you know what it's like to be me?" The last alternative in keeping boys involved in a successful learning process is by creating alternate programs to service them in times of conflict.

When young men are involved in negative actions that warrant immediate attention, rather than kicking them out of school to find more trouble to get involved in, create internal programs to address these matters. This can be done with resources that are already in the school, such as other students or possibly teachers during their breaks. Peer mediation among students has proven to be very effective, especially when it's structured properly and the right students are chosen to handle certain situations. This could also be an opportunity for students to earn extra privileges or incentives, which makes peer mediation attractive to other students, possibly even the ones who are going through mediation themselves. This is similar to when young men who once caused trouble become police officers to help prevent people like themselves from creating trouble.

If schools implemented programs for teachers to interact with students in their time of need, they could virtually eliminate out-of-school suspension altogether. With an investment in training a small group of teachers and providing an additional stipend for them, schools could actually receive more funding, since, by implementing this strategy, more students would be present during count days. The programs would also send an overall positive message to the student body.

In conjunction with the steps previously given, educators should consider strategies to keep boys interested in reading. A young man's reading level can impact his mental, physical, emotional, social, and financial future. Many studies show that most men in prison are poor readers, and that fact directly connects to the crimes they've committed.[28] This issue can be addressed by diagnosing and recognizing reading problems as early as possible because it identifies a misfortune that could cause future problems if it is overlooked. I've spoken to young men all over the country who have admitted that they are poor readers and feel forced to cause problems as a result of it.

Causing problems and being disruptive is their way of hiding and keeping the focus off the fact that they cannot read. This is why teachers should never attempt to force a young man to read out loud unless they're certain that his reading ability is up to par. When appropriate, it's very effective when teachers allow male students to pick their own reading material, if for no other reason than to see where their interests lie as well. Doing this also helps build confidence. In all educational settings, male students should be given the opportunity to incorporate visual and physical demonstrations in the learning process as often as possible. This is especially effective with reading because it helps them see exactly what's being taught. Sports, art, and other physical or visual activities should also be used to stimulate reading. This encourages students to read in a nonacademic environment.

If we're ever going to truly be an asset to our young men, we must meet them where they are instead of where we think they should be. We must always treat them with respect and understand that their worth is far greater than their worst act. As adults and leaders, we should compliment positive attitudes and behaviors at all times. We should be open and honest with youngsters and never make a promise we can't keep. Broken promises lead to distrust and disappointment, which sometimes encourages young men to avoid expecting anything from adults altogether, while becoming angry at the world in the process. Think about the young man who's mad at the world right now because his father told him he would be back but still hasn't returned, years later.

It's also in our best interest to use young men in positive leadership positions whenever possible and learn their language, while utilizing their ideas and perspectives when appropriate. As we have seen in countless situations, young men will force you to pay attention to them, even if it costs them their lives or yours. More importantly, when a support system of high standards and expectations is in place, they'll become the men society needs them to be.

In essence, there are five essentials that all young people need, especially young men. When one or more of these elements are missing, school shootings, gang and youth violence, teen pregnancy, school dropout rates, and disrespect toward parents and teachers will become more commonplace. On the other hand, when these essentials are present, it will result in healthy relationships, positive peer influence, improved grades, respect for adults, and higher high school and college graduation rates. My workshop "Winning back our Boys" is in high demand because of the basis of these five elements that I'll briefly discuss.

The first element I teach is the importance of unconditional love. To a degree this is self-explanatory because we understand the concept, but we don't realize how we undermine it by the things we say. Specific words cause young people to feel love when they … or if they … or because they…. These blanks can be filled in with a number of things, all of which young people feel the need to possess or do before they'll ever receive love.

The second element is emotional safety. This is probably the most ignored and misunderstood because emotions can be very complex. Our unconscious mind's top priority is to keep us emotionally safe, even if it means lying to ourselves. This is why young people will resort to something that's painful in order to avoid something else that they think will cause them even more pain.

The third element is a sense of belonging. This is why young people will change the way they dress, talk, and look just to fit into an environment that will give them a sense of belonging. The fourth element is importance and acceptance. They can go hand in hand, but there is a certain aspect that must be considered. You can accept someone without making them feel important, and you can also try and make someone feel important without accepting them. Young people need unconditional acceptance just as they need unconditional love. They may only feel accepted when they act like their sister, get good grades, grow taller, become what they think a man is, and the list goes on.

The last element is appreciation. Boys, as well as girls, need appreciation in the form of affection. There are many false perceptions surrounding this need—such as, boys don't need affection, or girls just need more affection—and they all come down to belief systems. In reality, boys are no less affectionate or emotional than girls are; it's just programming that causes boys to think they shouldn't be vulnerable, that they shouldn't cry or show emotions.

The five essentials are just the surface level. For the sake of time and space, I'm not able to elaborate on this segment of the workshop, which is complemented by a diagram that explains this further. However, I wanted to provide a few key pieces of information that adults can immediately put into practice to help them better understand specific behaviors of youth.

KEY POINTS FROM THIS CHAPTER

RESOURCES

1. http://www.manhattan-institute.org/html/cr_48.htm. 1-12-07
2. http://www.maec.org/achieve/1.html 1-13-07.
3. http://www.healing-arts.org/children/ADHD/. 1-13-07.
4. http://www.census.gov/Press-Release/www/releases/archives/facts_for_features_special_editions/001737.html. 1-11-07.
5. #8pg41. "Angry Young Men" Aaron Kipnis, PHD. San Francisco, CA, 1999.
6. #15pg33. "Right Brained children in a left brained world" Jeffrey Freed, M.A.T. and Laurie Parsons New York, NY, 1997.
7. http://www.livescience.com/strangenews/060718_illiterate_boys.html. 3-02-07
8. http://www.inmotionmagazine.com/peterz1.html. 2-17-07
9. U.S. Department of Education, 2002.
10. www.mea.org/ipd. December 1, 2005
11. http://www.cnn.com/US/9810/13/teacher.shortage/index.html. May 22, 2007
12. www.ritalindeath.com. May 25, 2007
13. Ebony, July 2006, page 154
14. Text of presentation given by Patti Johnson in October 1999.
15. #14pg135 "The boys and girls Learn differently action guide for teachers" Michael Gurian and Arlette C. Ballew, San Francisco, CA, 2003.
16. www.worldnewsstand.net/health/PSYCHiatry.htm. 12-12-05.
17. #6pg30pg18 "Media Unlimited" Todd Gitlin, 2001.

18. #2 pg80 "State of emergency we must save African American males," Jawanza Kunjufu, 2001.

19. http://www.justicepolicy.org/projects/investments/investments.htm. May 25, 2007.

20. www.dyslexia.com. 3-14-07..

21. gangsta411.com 1-10-07.

22. www.state.me.us/dhhs/bohdcfh/inj/fs_suicide.html. 8-7-06.

23. #1 pg65 "Why boys don't talk and why it matter,s" Susan Morris Shaffer & Linda Perlman Gordon, 2005.

24. U.S. Dept. of Justice, 2002b.

25. www.policemag.com. 3-16-07.

26. www.altereddimensions.net/crime/Ms13gang.htm. 3-16-07.

27. www.washingtonpost.com/wp-dyn/articles/a54899-2005.html. Jan6, 2007..

28. www.dioceseofnewark.orgcityrpt.htm 9-2-06.

29. http://english.people.com.cn/200503/03/eng20050303_175406.html. May 25, 2007.

30. http://www.juvenilejustice.com/prevention.html. May 25, 2007.

31. Raising Sons and Loving It!: Helping Your Boys Become Godly Men By Carrie Oliver, Gary J. Oliver.

32. http://forum.empireinteractive.com/default.aspxMID=66831B646DocTID=71ECFSA2-496A-4C82-B609-74A73B035B1F 3-25-07.

33. http://www.clydelewis.com/dis/curt/curt.html.. 3-17-07.

34. http://heathyminds.org/mediaviolence.cfm. 3-17-07.

35. www.babyandtoddlerville.com/home/content/view/167/29/. 2-13-2007.

36. http://students.tua.edu/rm/rmr6124/ppl.html. 2-06-07.

37. http://en.wikipedia.org/wiki/super_Columbine_Massacre_RPG%212-14. 3-13-07.

38. http://en.wikipedia.org/wiki/Dawson_college_shooting. 3-13-07.

39. www.medinstitute.org. May 27, 2007.
40. http://www.realchoices.com/teenfacts.html. May 27, 2007.
41. http://www.who.int/en/. May 15,2007.
42. hh://pureintimacy.org/gr/intimacy/understanding/a0000082.cfm. 3-17-07.
43. www.takingfire.com/drcarson. 3-25-07.
44. http://fathersforlife.org/divorce/chldrndiv.htm. May 16, 2007.
45. #10pgs31-32. "Restoring the Village, Values, and commitment," Juwanza Kunjufu, 1996.
46. http://ssw.unc.edu/fcrp/cspn/vol7_no1/understand_parents_prison.htm. May 16, 2007.
47. www.Abstinence.net. 2-3-2005.
48. http://www.isma.org.uk/stressnw/effcomm.htm. May 24, 2007.
49. http://mi-gender-equity.com/erfm/erfm.shtml. May 25, 2007.
50. http://www.gazette.net/stories/052307/montnew221126_32333.shtml
51. http://www.wagv.org/gun-violence.php
52. http://www.usatoday.com/tech/news/2006-01-08-MySpace-teens_x.htm
53. http://en.wikipedia.org/wiki/Video_game_controversy
54. www.sott.net/articles/show/142060-Brainwashed-into-Loyalty-British-intelligence-is-recruiting-adrenaline-addicted-video-games-junkies
55. http://cybervigilantes.blogspot.com/2007/10/technology-commentary-for-29th-october.html
56. http://www.sott.net/articles/show/142060-Brainwashed-into-Loyalty-British-intelligence-is-recruiting-adrenaline-addicted-video-games-junkies
57. http://cybervigilantes.blogspot.com/2007/10/technology-commentary-for-29th-october.html
58. http://cybervigilantes.blogspot.com/2007/10/technology-commentary-for-29th-october.html

ABOUT THE AUTHOR

Chris Cannon, acclaimed author of *WINNING back our BOYS* has quickly become recognized nationally as an in demand speaker for youth audiences and adults alike. Cannon has dedicated his life to improving the lives of young people "AT RISK". He developed his key insight into the lives of young people through extensive traveling and working with youth and community programs across the country. As a heartfelt speaker, paralleled with a former career as a high school teacher and coach, he's developed a reputation as one who effectively impacts today's youth and the adults who train them. After struggling to overcome the appealing temptations of sex, drugs, and other pressures as a college football player, he discovered his passion and purpose for helping youth overcome these same pressures. After just a few minutes with Chris, his genuine spirit and unique style of "teaching true leaders how to be more effective," will make you feel like you've known him your entire life. As a cross-cultural communicator, he speaks as if a generation depends on it, leaving audiences empowered and equipped with a sense of HOPE! This supports his philosophy; "The battle is not lost unless you accept defeat". He resides in San Antonio, TX.

RESOURCES I RECOMMEND

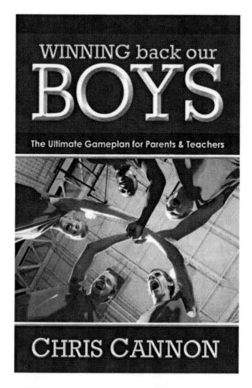

You've read the book, now hear the workshop live!

You'll discover:
- How to bring out the leadership qualities in every young man, regardless of their current or pass behavior.
- The 5 essential feelings all young men seek, that will positively transform their behaviors today.
- The 6 layers of emotions that will determine the outcome of every young person's future.
- How to help behaviorally challenged boys become the example for others to follow.
- Why boys focus more on athletics than academics and how schools encourage it.
- The most effective way to discipline young men and why thy'll love you for it!
- And so much more...

Go to **www.Fighting4Youth.com** and schedule this workshop!

THE 10 SECRETS OF DISCIPLINE THAT ALL YOUTH DESIRE!

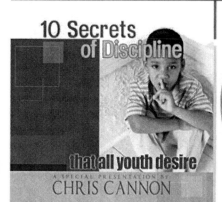

What you'll discover:

- The two ways young people communicate to adults and the most effective response to eliminate conflict and produce positive results.
- How to say what you mean, mean what you say, and get what you want.
- How to get youth to do what you want, even if it's something they don't want without punishing them.
- How to get youth to discipline themselves and take responsibility without blaming the adults in their lives.
- How to recognize what youth are asking for through their behavior and how to respond with the right answer.
- The #1 way to get children to assist you in disciplining them.
- And so much more...

What you'll discover in secrets #4 and #10 is worth more than 4X the $10 investment for the entire CD.

Go to *www.Fighting4Youth.com* **NOW and book Chris to speak live!**

"A WHALE OF A SMILE"

DR. LOREN D. ALVES, D.M.D.
PEDIATRIC DENTISTRY - BOARD CERTIFIED

- INFANTS
- CHILDREN
- ADOLESCENTS
- HOSPITAL DENTISTRY

SE HABLA ESPAÑOL!

1954 EAST HOUSTON, SUITE #210
SAN ANTONIO, TX 78202
MONDAY (HOSPITAL)
TUESDAY THRU FRIDAY 8:30 AM - 5:00 PM
MOST INSURANCES & MEDICAID
CALL US TODAY (210) 208-6525
WWW.AWHALEOFASMILE.COM

LaVergne, TN USA
22 March 2010
176809LV00001B/7/P